Scholastic World Cultures Program

THE SOVIET UNION AND EASTERN EUROPE

by Hope T. Ludlow

Consultants
ROGER PAXTON, Ph.D.
Associate Professor of History
University of Utah

ALBERT SERETNY, Ph.D.
Supervisor of Social Studies K-12
New Haven, Conn., Public Schools

Readability Consultant
LAWRENCE B. CHARRY, Ed.D.

SCHOLASTIC BOOK SERVICES
New York Toronto London Sydney Auckland

Other Titles in This Series

THE INDIAN SUBCONTINENT
LATIN AMERICA
SOUTHEAST ASIA
THE MIDDLE EAST
TROPICAL AND SOUTHERN AFRICA
CHINA

Copyright © 1973 by Scholastic Magazines, Inc.
All rights reserved.
Published by Scholastic Book Services,
a division of Scholastic Magazines, Inc.
Printed in the U.S.A.
16 15 14 13 12 11 10 9 8 7 6 5   6 7 8 9/7 0 1/8

03

Hope T. Ludlow is a former editor for Scholastic Book Services who has traveled widely in the Soviet Union and in the various nations of Eastern Europe. She is presently an editor with the Conference Board Record *as well as a free-lance writer on economics matters.*

General Editor for WORLD CULTURES PROGRAM: *Stephen M. Lewin*
Associate Editor: John Nickerson
Associate Editor: LeRoy Hayman
Teaching Guide Editor: Frances Plotkin

Book and Cover Designer: Irmgard Lochner
Photo Editor: Elnora Bode
Production Editor: Nancy Smith

COVER: Moscow's Red Square is alive with banners, posters, and thousands of people celebrating one of the major holidays of communism, May Day. In the background, the gleaming domes of Old Russia's St. Basil's church, built in the 16th century, soar over the modern-day celebration.

THE
SOVIET UNION
AND
EASTERN EUROPE

Table of Contents

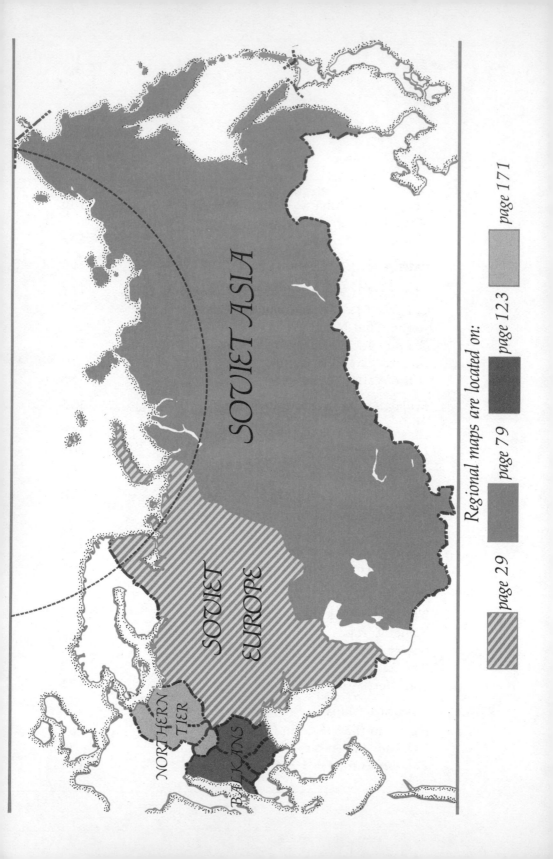

Regional maps are located on:

page 29   page 79   page 123   page 171

*❧ "This does not mean that we
bring back from Moscow
the promise of instant peace,
but we do bring back
the beginning of a process
that can lead to lasting peace."*

PRESIDENT RICHARD NIXON
ON RETURNING FROM THE
SOVIET UNION AND POLAND, 1972.

PROLOGUE

A NEW
BEGINNING

A FEW YEARS AGO, a young Soviet couple named Nina and Alexei* left their home in a large Soviet city and traveled to the southwestern corner of Soviet Siberia. As recent graduates in agricultural science,

---

*See Glossary for pronunciation guide.

they were offered jobs as managers on a new farm located on the dry, windy Siberian plateau.

Wheat was to be the main crop of the new farm. The first harvest was large. Government agricultural officials in Moscow, capital of the Soviet Union, were so pleased with the size of the crop that first year that they ordered production levels doubled in the second year.

Nina and Alexei thought it unwise to try to grow two large crops, one after the other, without a year's rest for the soil. But they had been ordered to grow the crops, so they did. The second year's harvest was smaller than the first. The officials told them to try again. The third harvest was even smaller than the second because the earth had not had time to store up the infrequent rains, and the topsoil had dried out and mostly blown away.

Nina and Alexei were disappointed with their Siberian farming experience. They were angry that they had been given so little control over the planting programs. The fourth consecutive harvest yielded even less grain, and the agricultural officials still refused to let the land "rest." So Nina and Alexei decided to leave Siberia.

A friend told them of an opening in the central Asian section of the Soviet Union known as Kazakhstan.* This area is mostly desert. Only in the northern part of Kazakhstan, where Nina and Alexei settled, is the land suitable for farming.

At first farming was as difficult here as it had been in Siberia. No large crops had ever before grown here. But hundreds of students came in summer. They helped plow the new fields, mix plaster, carry heavy stones for walls of buildings, and make mud bricks.

For relaxation there was a dance at the meeting hall, a movie, or singing to the strummed *balalaika*,*

⌇§ Communism is the political and economic system that governs these nations — right down to the personal lives of their citizens.

---

a Russian guitar. Nina and Alexei often invited friends to their small flat-roofed house. And sometimes Nina would offer them pieces of *non*,* the crusty Asian bread she learned to bake in the earthen oven outside the house.

After several years of irrigating and cultivating the soil, the new farm was considered a success. Nina and Alexei felt that their training was being put to good use. So they made up their minds to stay in Soviet central Asia.

☆　☆　☆　☆　☆　☆　☆　☆　☆

Nina and Alexei are just two of the many people you will meet in this book. Their stories help tell what is happening today in the Soviet Union and the various nations of Eastern Europe. The stories will not, however, show all the varieties of life-styles, traditions, and values held by people in this part of the world. The area is just too vast and too varied for that. But the experiences of Nina and Alexei are similar in many ways to what is happening to other young people throughout the Soviet Union and Eastern Europe. For all over the region, young people are caught up in the sweep of change.

Another thing that links the people of this region is communism. Communism is the political and economic system that governs these nations — right down to the personal lives of their citizens. Nina and Alexei are affected by the Communist government of

11

the Soviet Union in many ways that might seem strange to a citizen of a non-Communist country. It was the Communist government which controlled their education, decided that they would get advanced training, sent them to the new farm in Siberia, told them what crops to grow and how much, and sent them to central Asia when they wanted to leave Siberia.

So no study of the life-styles and culture of the peoples of the Soviet Union and Eastern Europe can fail to take account of the enormous role of communism in people's daily lives. But the fact that communism plays a part in the everyday lives of people does not mean that it is a failure or that most of the people of the Communist world are unhappy with their governments. The Soviet Union, for one, has made enormous strides in many areas in the half century plus that communism has been in power. Most of the Soviet people seem to be satisfied with their nation's progress. Most feel they are far better off than they were under the czars* (The title "czar" comes from the Latin word *Caesar*. It might be compared to the title "emperor."), who ruled Russia before the Communists took control.

In Eastern Europe, communism has shallower roots. The eight countries of Eastern Europe are: Albania,* Bulgaria,* Czechoslovakia,* East Germany, Hungary, Poland, Rumania,* and Yugoslavia.* They are all latecomers to communism. It was not until after the end of World War II in 1945 that communism took over in these eight countries.

Being somewhat new to communism may be one reason why many of these countries are sometimes shaky in their devotion to the Soviet brand of communism. For some years the Soviet Union expected the smaller Communist nations of Eastern Europe to follow the Soviet lead unquestioningly. Now several of these countries are no longer content to revolve like satellites around the planet Moscow. They want to determine their own futures. They want to adapt communism — or even another system of government perhaps — to their own needs.

Today a new generation is growing up in the Soviet Union and Eastern Europe. The future seems promising to these young people, but they will demand more of life than their parents did. The changes they will help make are of the utmost importance to us. For it is this generation, coming of age today, that will direct the course of a group of nations that makes up one of the major forces in the modern world.

1
ROOTS OF SOVIET CULTURE

Chapter 1

The Land

DOES THE SOVIET UNION lie halfway around the world from the United States? Or are the two nations separated by only a few miles?

The answer to both questions is "yes."

The Soviet Union does lie halfway around the world from the United States. The 90 degrees *west* longitude line runs right down through Wisconsin, Illinois, and Mississippi in the middle of the U.S. If you could cut straight down from 90 degrees west through the center of the earth and come out the other side, you would be on the 90 degrees *east* longitude line. This line passes through the heart of Siberia in Soviet Asia. These two lines are half a world apart.

But the Soviet Union and the U.S. are also next-door neighbors. At the Bering Strait, easternmost Soviet Siberia almost nudges the coast of American

◄§ Winter is the longest season in most of the Soviet Union. For about half the year, all plant life sleeps and people's lives slow down.

Alaska. Only about two miles apart are Big Diomede* Island, a Soviet possession, and Little Diomede Island, an offshore part of Alaska. In fact, the mainlands of Siberia and Alaska are only 51 miles from each other across the Strait.

The Soviet Union is the largest country in area in the world. It occupies one sixth of the earth's land surface. Its area is larger than the moon's. It is more than 20 times the size of the eight other Communist countries of Eastern Europe and more than double the size of the 50 states of the United States. From the Bering Sea on the east to the Baltic Sea on the west, the Soviet Union sprawls across some 6,000 miles.

Three fourths of the Soviet Union lies in Asia, making it the largest country on that continent. Yet the one fourth that lies in Europe is almost as large as all the rest of Europe combined.

Within this huge country are generous samplings of nearly all of the earth's geographical features. It has Arctic icelands and subtropical forests; tumbling rivers and crystal-clear lakes; desert wastes and rich, black croplands; towering mountains and broad plains. Except for rubber, it has practically all the important raw materials needed for modern industrial development.

Land in large measure helps shape the lives of the people who inhabit it. It influences how they earn

Physical fitness is important in the Soviet Union. In snow and cold, these Moscovites exercise.

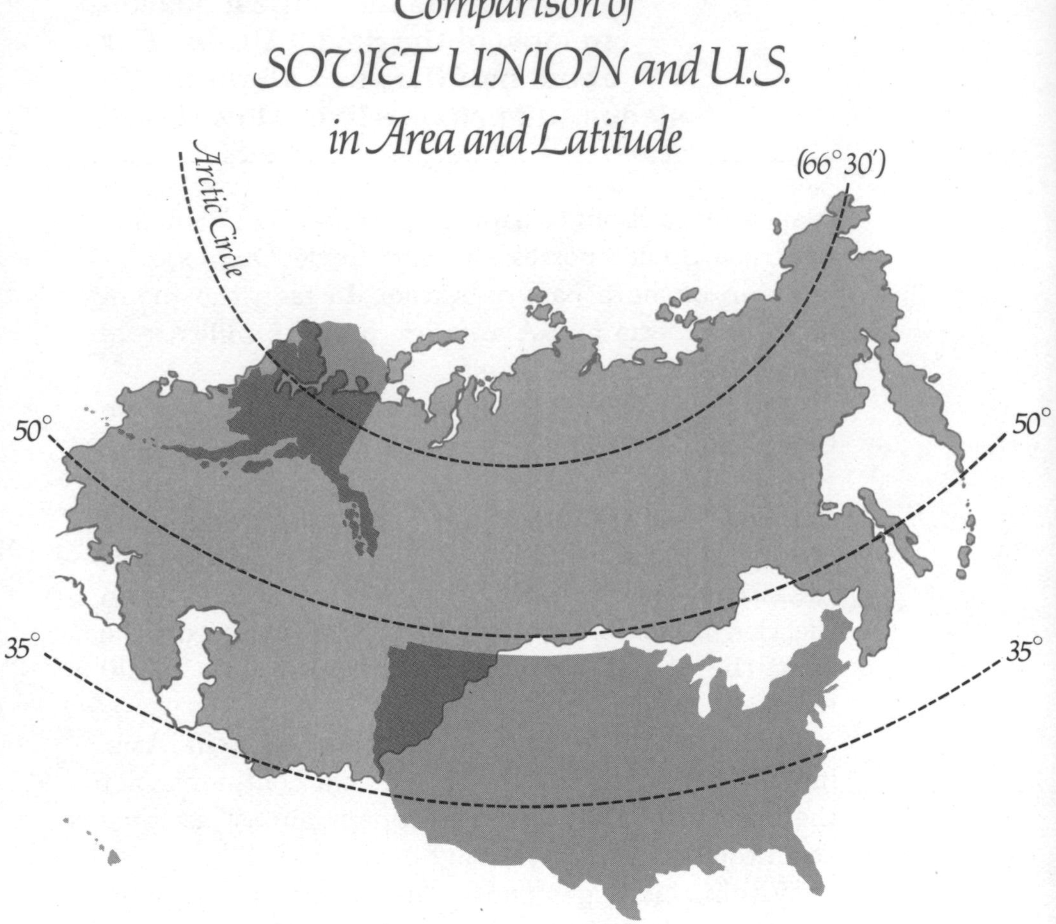

Comparison of
SOVIET UNION and U.S.
in Area and Latitude

Arctic Circle

(66° 30')

50°   50°

35°   35°

their livings and how they exist from day to day, from season to season, from generation to generation.

But life is also partially shaped by climate. Almost all of the Soviet Union is located in latitudes well north of the "lower 49" states of the United States. If the Soviet Union could somehow be picked up in one piece and placed in the Western Hemisphere, Moscow would be somewhere in the Hudson Bay region of Canada and Leningrad would be in Alaska (*see* map above).

Thus winter is the longest season in most of the Soviet Union. For about half the year, all plant life sleeps and people's lives slow down. Summers are warm but short. Spring and autumn are even shorter.

To get from one end of the Soviet Union to the other, we could jet across its vast land in considerably less than 24 hours. (But we might be confused by having to change our watches every time we passed through one of the 11 time zones in the Soviet Union.) Traveling by train is much slower, but it gives us a fine first-time glimpse of the land and its people. So let's choose a rail trip.

Our train runs along the Trans-Siberian Railroad, and our departure point is at its eastern end, the city of Nakhodka.* This is a port 70 miles east of Vladivostok,* the Soviet Union's major naval base on the Sea of Japan. The journey will be a long one. It will take nearly eight days to get to Moscow by rail, with more than 80 stops along the way.

So we settle down and make ourselves comfortable. The porter tells us that meals will be served in the dining car. Dishes might include cabbage soup (shchi*), roast chicken, small steaks, eggs, black bread, and many other foods. At the train stops, we have the chance to rush into the station to buy radishes, cucumbers, cold chicken, or other snacks. Or we can order the train attendant to serve us tea from a *samovar,** or urn, and lemon cookies.

But eating (and sleeping) does not take all our time. Outside the car window is an endlessly fascinating view. For the first several days of the journey, the Trans-Siberian rail route passes through the Siberian woodlands, mainly pine, spruce, and birch.

The Siberian forests, called *taiga,** are deep and dense. They extend south for about 150 miles from the rail line and north for more than 1,200 miles.

19

North of the taiga is the vast Arctic and sub-Arctic tundra, where no trees grow and the earth a little below the surface is permanently frozen. South of the taiga is prairie, and south of that is desert. The Soviet taiga alone covers an area almost as large as the United States. Unfortunately for Soviet lumbermen, it is difficult to float out the taiga's timber to where it can be used. This is because the rivers that drain the taiga all flow north — into Arctic bays and seas which remain frozen most of the year.

The rail line runs right through the taiga. It is just about the only way to get people in, and logs out, of this immense green wilderness. Dirt roads are few and short, and paved roads are even fewer and shorter. But here and there along the railroad are small settlements, with log houses surrounded by plowed fields.

As the train moves north and then westward, good-sized cities begin to appear on the horizon. These cities have sprung up only in recent times. They were created to make use of the mineral resources of the land or the hydroelectric potential of the rivers. They include communities with, to Westerners, jaw-cracking names like Khabarovsk* and Novosibirsk.*

Despite the presence of such cities, eastern Siberia remains a vast and lonely place. The taiga is still virgin forest for millions of acres, and only the trappers know even a small part of it. They go into the woodlands in search of pelts — bear, wolf, mink, fox, and the rare and costly Russian sable.

After Novosibirsk the land begins to change. The forests diminish, and treeless prairies, or *steppes*,* emerge. The steppes are almost as vast as the taiga. Those that remain unplowed are covered with tall grasses. But many steppes are cultivated. Fields of

POPULATION DISTRIBUTION IN THE SOVIET UNION

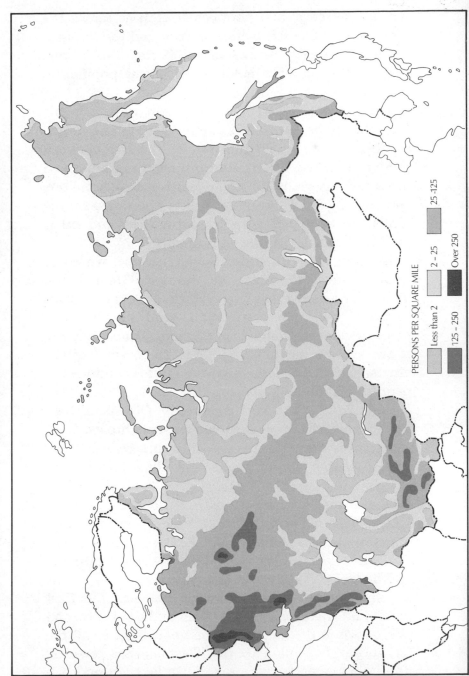

PERSONS PER SQUARE MILE

Less than 2	2 – 25	25 - 125
125 – 250	Over 250	

wheat, rye, corn, and potatoes stretch as far as the eye can see. The soil is more fertile and the living is somewhat easier in western Siberia. That's one reason why the area holds a far bigger population than does eastern Siberia.

From the level steppes, our train rolls into the foothills of the Ural* Mountains. This is the north-south mountain chain that marks the line between Soviet Asia and Soviet Europe. Deep within these mountains is great mineral wealth — coal, iron ore, copper, bauxite (aluminum ore). The cities of the Urals are equipped with blast furnaces and other facilities to turn the ores into metals.

Crossing the Urals into Soviet Europe, we come upon a countryside much like America's Great Plains. The fields are covered with rye, wheat, and oats. Cattle graze in the grassy areas. The land is dotted with peasant villages, from which farmers go out each day to work in the surrounding fields. In contrast to the almost-deserted Siberia, here the land is comfortably peopled and under human control.

Still, farming this land is not easy. Dry spells, heat waves, and cold snaps are ever-present threats. Over most of the Soviet Union the only sure weather prediction is that winter snows will come early — and stay late.

One of the last train stops is Kuibyshev,* on the Volga* River. The 2,300-mile Volga is a busy commercial inland waterway, and Kuibyshev has many docks and piers to accommodate the river traffic.

The Volga is only one of many rivers and canals in a network of water highways between the Caspian* and Black seas in the south and the Baltic and White seas in the north. Half again as large as all the Great Lakes combined, the Caspian Sea (which, despite its name, is not a sea, but a lake) supports a

LAND USE IN THE SOVIET UNION

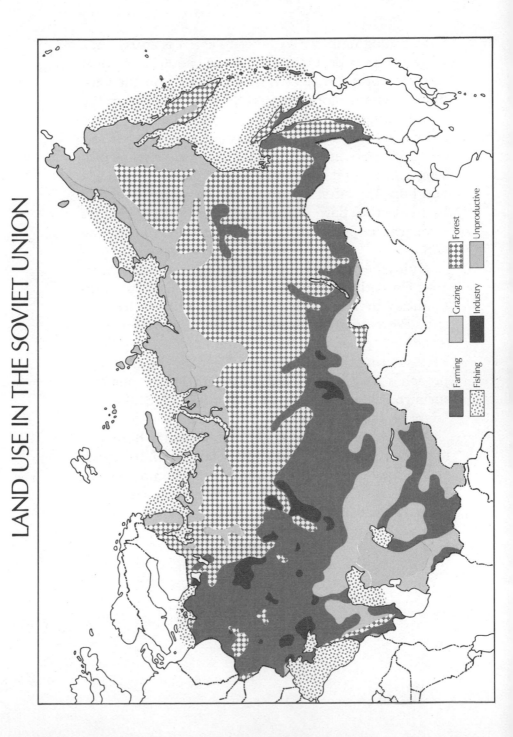

Forest
Unproductive
Grazing
Industry
Farming
Fishing

huge fishing industry. A favorite catch is sturgeon, a large fish that provides the Soviet people with most of their world-famous caviar. At Baku,* on the Caspian's western shore, oil rigs stand girder-deep in the sea, drawing up tankersfull of "black gold."

Up and down the waterways of the Volga, Don, and Dvina* rivers go an unending procession of passenger boats and freighters, fishing craft, oil tankers, and huge log rafts. Rivers are also a major source of hydroelectric power, although the Soviet Union's electrical output is still far smaller than that of the U.S.

Kuibyshev is only a day's train journey from Moscow. On both sides of the tracks are industrial communities that feed their products into the capital city. Between these factory towns are stretches of woodland, green in the short summers, hung with icicles during the long winters. Then, as the train approaches Moscow, it passes through long strings of surburbs where apartment buildings stand close to factories and warehouses.

Moscow at last! We might change trains here and take the crack Red Arrow express north to Leningrad. Or we may care to travel another 14 hours west to Minsk* and the Polish frontier. Whatever we do, in Moscow we can at least get off the train, stretch our legs, and meet more of the Soviet people.

Chapter 2

The Soviet Peoples

UNLIKE, SAY, NEW YORK OR PARIS, Moscow is not an international capital. That is, it does not play host to many visitors from foreign countries. The Soviet Union opens its doors to relatively few tourists, and those who do come are given carefully supervised tours.

In another sense, however, Moscow is a world capital — for the Soviet world. Indeed, the Soviet Union is almost a world in itself, full of variety and contrast. For example, in medicine, science, and technology, the Soviet Union is taking giant steps toward the 21st century. But over vast areas of the countryside, it is still struggling to get into the 20th century. It is a country of great natural wealth, but it is also one of constant shortages. In some things its Communist government is a model of efficiency and in others, a mess of bureaucratic bungling.

About half the population of the Soviet Union is made up of people called Russians. The remainder

People of many different ethnic origins mix in the Soviet Union. For example, the girls above are from Leningrad in Soviet Europe. The girl at right is a young Moslem from the city of Bukhara in Soviet central Asia.

is divided into a bewildering assortment of nationalities ranging down the alphabet from Abazas* to Yukagirs.*

What is a nationality? This is a difficult thing to pin down precisely. A nationality, as the Soviets think of it, could be a people who all speak the same language. But people who speak the same language might be of different nationalities because their customs or religions are different. It is a feeling of "uniqueness" that makes a nationality — common language, religion, or customs.

The Russians, along with two other Soviet nationalities, the Ukrainians* and the Byelorussians,* are a mixture of peoples who are called Slavic.* The Slavs moved out of the region between the Vistula*

The Soviet people are divided into a bewildering assortment of nationalities, ranging down the alphabet from Abazas to Yukagirs.

and Dnieper* rivers (see map, page 29) about 13 or 14 centuries ago. Some split off and settled in what is now Poland, Yugoslavia, Bulgaria, and Czechoslovakia; and their descendants today make up most of the population of these countries. Others traveled to the Dnieper and the Upper Volga river regions of what is today the Soviet Union. This group later became known as the "Great Russians."

As the most numerous nationality in the Soviet Union, the Russians dominate the political, cultural, and economic life of the country. As a result, "Russia" and "Russians" are often used as short — but inaccurate — titles for the whole of the Soviet Union and all its people.

Actually, Russia (or, as it is officially called, the Russian Soviet Federated Socialist Republic) is only one of the 15 "republics" which make up the Soviet Union. The republics are something like U.S. states, each with its own government and some authority over local affairs. There are also a Ukrainian Soviet Socialist Republic, a Byelorussian Soviet Socialist Republic, and 12 other "Soviet Socialist Republics" (see maps on pages 29 and 79). Together the 15 republics are called the Union of Soviet Socialist Republics — the U.S.S.R. or the Soviet Union for short.

In theory, members of any ethnic group may live wherever they please. But most of them tend to live together, sticking to their traditional communities. In central Asia, for example, there are large numbers of Moslem peoples, descendants of nomads who roamed the southern steppes for centuries without regard to boundaries. This way of life came to an end within the last century, as Russia, Iran, Afghanistan, and China set down firm national boundaries.

In recent years, the Soviet government has built industries and schools in its Moslem areas. Today the

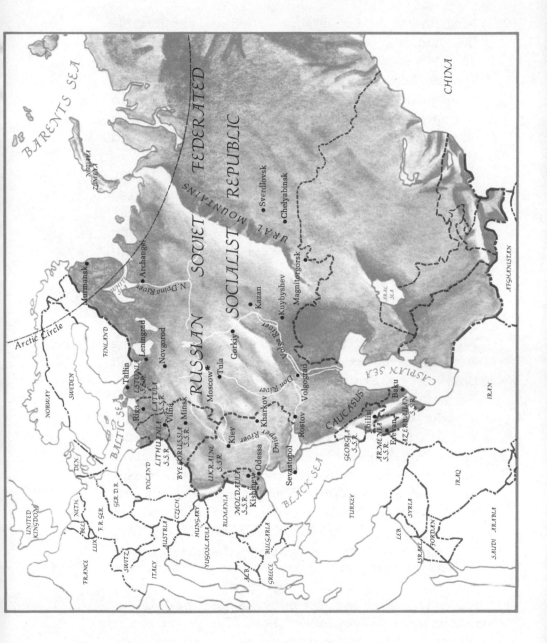

Moslem peoples live a more settled and comfortable life than ever before in their history. Still, old ways and old values remain strong, and a visitor to the area will see bearded men wearing turbans and flowing robes mixing freely with people in Western dress. In the open bazaars of the cities, men wearing Moslem skull caps sell vegetables, figs, and spices much as their ancestors did centuries ago.

The southwestern section of the Soviet Union, a mountainous area known as the Caucasus,* has much mineral wealth and a mild, sunny climate. And, like the climate, the people of the Caucasus are friendly, outgoing, and neighborly. The major nationality groups of the Caucasus are the Georgians,* the Azerbaijanis,* and the Armenians.*

The Baltic peoples of the northwest are neighbors to the Russians, but have a very different culture. Most Russians, if they are religious, belong to the Russian Orthodox Church. Most Estonians* and Latvians* are Protestant, and most Lithuanians* are Roman Catholic. The Russian language is written in a script called Cyrillic,* but all three Baltic languages are written in the Latin script, the one we use for writing English. For centuries, Estonia, Latvia, and Lithuania were fought over by Poland, Russia, and Sweden. After World War I, the three tiny Baltic nations won their independence. But this period was short-lived, and in 1940, during World War II, they were taken over and annexed into the Soviet Union.

Many Soviet ethnic groups do not have their own "republic." They include large numbers of German-speaking and Polish-speaking people, as well as nearly three million Soviet Jews. The plight of the Soviet Jews has aroused the world's attention in recent years. For centuries before the Russian Revolution of 1917, the Jews of Russia were persecuted.

They were forced to live in special sections of cities called *ghettos*,* and subjected to cruel *pogroms** (organized massacres). Some relief came with the Revolution.

But after the Revolution the pressure on the Jews was of a subtler sort. Their way was sometimes blocked in job advancement, in appointment to government posts, in admission to college. Religious worship was discouraged; and Jewish newspapers, theaters, and cultural groups were suppressed. In the past few years many Jews who wanted to leave the Soviet Union for Israel were either not allowed to go, or forced to pay a high tax in order to depart. (For that matter, very few other Soviet citizens were allowed to leave either.)

Religious Jews are not the only ones who have been discouraged from practicing their faith. Karl Marx, the founder of communism, believed that "religion is the opium of the people." When the Soviets came to power in 1917, they began a policy of opposing all religions.

Under the czars, the official religion in Russia was the Russian Orthodox Church. After the Revolution, the Communists destroyed many cathedrals and churches and turned others into museums, public meeting halls, and storehouses. They tried to wipe out all religion in the Soviet Union.

The Orthodox Church still exists, but it has lost all its political influence. The plight of the Church has improved somewhat in recent years, but religion is still largely restricted. The Soviet authorities oppose religion as being dangerous and unscientific. But because religious belief is still strong, the authorities have hesitated to completely ban the practice of religion. Allowing a certain amount of worship to go on is good propaganda.

31

*Ancient prints shows Varangians from Scandinavia cross-
ing the sea to begin conquest of some of the Slavic people.*

IN THE BEGINNING

SLAVIC PEOPLES — Russians, Ukrainians, and Byelorussians — make up the great majority of the Soviet popula-

tion. It was the Slavs who helped build one of the first great empires of Russia.

In the ninth century the Slavic people lived in and around two communities — Novgorod* in the northwest and Kiev* in the southwest. Both cities lay along an almost continuous chain of rivers and lakes that reached from the Baltic Sea in the north to the Black Sea in the south.

Along the Baltic lived the Scandinavian Northmen, who were also called Vikings, or Varangians.* They were bold and warlike sailors, eager to conquer wealthier lands. And one of the wealthiest of all cities in the ninth century was Constantinople,* capital of the Byzantine* Empire. The quickest way to Constantinople from the Baltic was along the water route that runs by Novgorod and Kiev.

The Varangians sailed south and attacked Constantinople. Although they did not capture it, they took ransom from the city. But, more important, some of the Varangians — liking what they had seen on their way south — settled among the Slavs. They learned the Slavic language, adopted Slavic ways, and became farmers instead of fighters.

In about the year A.D. 862, according to legend, the Slavs chose Rurik,* a Varangian prince, as their leader. Rurik's own tribe was the Rus, and the territory around Novgorod soon became known as the Land of the Rus, or Russia.

Rurik's kinsman, Oleg, succeeded him. Oleg set up his court in Kiev, which historians now call "the mother of Russian cities." Under Oleg's descendants the territory of Kiev Rus stretched from the Baltic Sea to the Black Sea, from the Volga River on the east to the Danube* River on the west.

All this time the Rus kept on trading with Constantinople. There they saw the wealth of the Byzantine Empire — its lavish architecture, its sumptuous jewels and silks, its rich bazaars. They saw the magnificent Church of St. Sophia in Constantinople, where people of the Greek Orthodox faith, a branch of Christianity, worshiped. And they were impressed by the beauty of Christianity, so

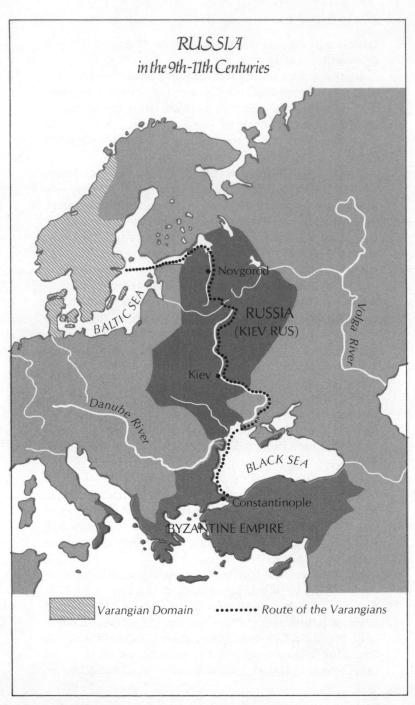

RUSSIA
in the 9th-11th Centuries

Novgorod

RUSSIA
(KIEV RUS)

Volga River

BALTIC SEA

Danube River

Kiev

BLACK SEA

Constantinople

BYZANTINE EMPIRE

Varangian Domain ·········· Route of the Varangians

different from their simple pagan beliefs. Over the years, many Rus became Orthodox Christians. In A.D. 988 this creed became the official religion of Kiev Rus.

The same Greek monks who helped bring Christianity to Russia also brought an alphabet. The Russians, who until then had no alphabet, could now write their language. This was the Cyrillic alphabet, still in use today.

The power and importance of Kiev Rus began to decline in the mid-1000's. About 200 years later it fell to the conquering Mongolian armies under Genghis Khan* and later his grandson, Khan Batu.* Mounted on swift ponies, the Mongol warriors swept across Asia and central Russia. Mongol archers were deadly shots. In attacking the wooden cities of the Rus, the Mongols threw oil-filled clay pots with burning fuses that set off huge blazes.

The Mongols held Russia for more than two centuries. They plundered and destroyed and collected heavy taxes under the threat of outright butchery. Gradually, however, the Mongol hold on Russia grew weaker, and the native Russian princes began to regain control of their lands. In time a new city replaced Kiev as the leading Russian city. Its name was Moscow (see page 75).

It was Moscow's Grand Duke Ivan* III who ended Mongol rule in 1480 by refusing to pay taxes. For this he was called Ivan the Great. He gathered Russian princes and their lands under him, and assumed authority over the Russian Orthodox Church.

His grandson, Ivan IV, was the first ruler to be crowned, not as Grand Duke of Moscow but as czar of all Russia. Ivan IV is known in history as Ivan the Terrible. It is a name he well deserved. Brutal, hostile, and perhaps mad, he conducted a reign of terror in which he murdered hundreds of princes and landowners. He seized their estates and doled out the land to his followers. In a fit of rage, he even killed his oldest son.

The seized estates were valueless without the peasants who farmed the land. So Ivan and the czars that followed him passed decrees which forbade the peasants to leave the estates on which they worked. The peasants were called *serfs*, and serfdom was a form of slavery.

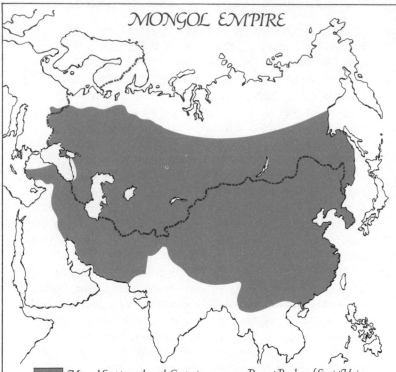

MONGOL EMPIRE

■ Mongol Empire, 13th - 15th Centuries   ▬▬ Present Borders of Soviet Union

After Ivan's death in 1584, a series of weak rulers and false claimants quarreled over Russia's throne. From 1604 to 1613 the country was torn apart by civil war and invasions. It is a period now remembered as the Time of Troubles. Finally, in 1613, a council of many classes of people from many regions elected a noble named Michael Romanov* as czar. The Romanovs would rule Russia for the next three centuries. They would be the last czars of Russia.

Under the first Romanovs, Russia extended its rule southward into the Ukraine and eastward across Siberia all the way to the Pacific. In 1682 the greatest Romanov, Peter I, became czar at the age of 10.

Everything about Peter was large. He was toweringly tall (close to seven feet), keenly intelligent, and restless. He could be exceedingly brutal. But he was eager to learn — and to use that learning to help his backward country. Peter traveled across Western Europe in disguise, observing how it had progressed while Russia stood still. In England and Holland he worked as a laborer in shipyards.

Peter was determined to follow Western Europe's example. So he returned home and moved his capital from Moscow to a new city named St. Petersburg. This would be his "window on the West."

Peter built ships, factories, and schools. He made Russian men shave off their long beards to look like the men of Western Europe. He imported skilled craftsmen from Western Europe and sent young Russians to Western Europe to learn crafts and skills.

Ideas new to Russia came through this "window on the West" and continued to do so after Peter's death in 1725. A regular army and navy were formed. A new calendar was introduced. The first Russian newspaper was published, and the first Russian theater was organized. But not all the new ideas would have been pleasing to Peter. Some nobles accepted Western ideas about liberty and social reform. And these ideas began slowly sifting down to some of the middle classes.

In the 1770's the serfs revolted. They were protesting the cruel treatment that forced them to work until they dropped, to be flogged until they fainted, often to be sold and separated from their families. The revolt, which spread over much of Russia, was finally put down by the troops of Empress Catherine II.

In many ways Catherine was also a great ruler. She too was influenced by the new ideas from the West. She sponsored schools and hospitals, encouraged women's education, introduced smallpox vaccination. But like Peter the Great, her attitude toward opposition remained intolerant and rigid. And she did not apply her liberal ideas to the serfs.

Catherine died in 1796. It would take almost a century and a quarter before a revolt of the peasants and workers turned Russia upside down. But talk of revolution was already in the air.

Chapter 3

Soviet Government and Economy

BOTH ENVIRONMENT AND TRADITION have had a part in shaping the values and culture of the Soviet peoples. The long, bitter winters have helped to mold a tough and proud people. A deep attachment to their vast land leaves a sense of pride in everything connected with "Mother Russia."

But no one can understand the Soviet people today without taking into account the effects of more than half a century of Communist rule. For under communism practically everything and everyone have been harnessed to the goals of the state.

Although the Soviet Union is a Communist nation, only about four or five percent of the Soviet people are actually members of the Communist Party. Unlike U.S. political parties, the Communist Party does not try to get everyone to belong. It aims to

Until recently, the Soviet economy was geared for "heavy industry," not consumer goods. Now, Soviet consumers demand — and get — more.

limit its membership to the most convinced believers in communism. Students prepare for membership through youth groups. Only the best of these students become Party members.

Applicants for Party membership must be at least 18 years old, and be recommended by at least three members of the local Party unit the applicant wishes to join. Approval as a full member takes a year. The Party carefully tests the loyalty of its members, new and old.

The Party structure is something like a pyramid. At its base are several hundred thousand local units, headquartered in factories, farms, offices, and schools throughout the Soviet Union. At the next level is the regional congress. Then comes the republic congress, the highest level in each of the 15 republics. Above

39

it is the all-union Party congress. Each level elects members to the level above itself.

The all-union Party congress elects the powerful Central Committee of the Communist Party, which in turn selects the Presidium. This is the most powerful Communist body in the U.S.S.R. It sets broad policies for the country which the Soviet government must carry out. There is a president of the Soviet Union, but he holds a largely figurehead position. The most powerful person in the Soviet Union is the General Secretary of the Party's Central Committee.

One reason for his great authority is that his is the only legal political party in the Soviet Union. And the Communist Party puts up only one candidate for each office. So an "election" means merely a rubber-stamp approval of the Party's nominee.

Thus the Communist Party runs the government of the U.S.S.R. — and the government runs the country. It runs the farms, the factories, the schools, the transportation systems, the banks, the apartment houses, the publishing houses, the broadcasting companies, and virtually every other part of the country's economic, cultural, and social life.

Of course, capitalist countries like the United States have some elements of government control and planning in their economy. In general, however, production in non-Communist nations is determined by the supply of goods, consumer demand, and other forces of the "free market." But in Communist states, almost all economic activities are planned and controlled by the government.

Workers labor in government-owned factories. Farmers plow and plant on government-owned or government-regulated farms. Consumers buy at

Women work alongside men on the construction of this Moscow apartment-house complex.

≈§ Soviet women often work in
jobs that in other countries
are considered "men's work"—
construction work, for example.

state-operated stores. The bulk of all income, of course, goes to the national government which, in turn, uses the money as it sees fit.

There is very little in the way of economic competition in the Soviet Union. The government decides what is to be produced, how much is to be produced, and what price it will cost.

In an effort to create an industrially strong Soviet Union, the Communist government has insisted that "heavy industry" come first. This means that top priority is given to steelmaking, power plants, industrial machinery, and other activities basic to the country's industrial development.

But an economy, even one so large as the Soviet Union's, can concentrate on just so many things at one time. Giving priority to one part of the economy means neglecting others. In the past, Soviet "light industry" that produces consumer goods — what people eat, use, and wear — has taken second place.

Thus many residents of Soviet cities live in tiny, crowded apartments, and few have their own homes. Most families have electric refrigerators, but few have cars. Those with cars usually keep them parked at special lots during the week and use them only on weekends. Cars are expensive, and gasoline is scarce. Store counters often have few goods, and people may line up for hours on the news — or rumor — that a shipment of, say, shoes is expected in.

Usually every adult member of a family goes to work, including the mother, unless she is pregnant or nursing a child. Four out of five Soviet women hold jobs outside the home. They receive the same pay as men and often work in jobs that in other countries are considered "men's work" — construction work, for example.

After a hard day's work, the people of the cities

Good Soviet workers are awarded all-expenses-
paid vacations. Here two factory employees
play chess on the beach of a Black Sea resort.

like to stroll down the broad boulevards (even in midwinter), gazing into shop windows. In the past few years, Soviet shoppers have had more to gaze at. Many Soviet families can now buy the most prized of all appliances — an electric refrigerator or a television set.

Until recently the Soviet economy has managed to provide its people with the basic necessities, but not too much more. It's rare that anyone starves in the

43

Soviet Union these days, and people did starve when Russia was ruled by the czars. But the usual Soviet diet is heavy on starchy foods, such as potatoes and bread, and is light on meat and dairy products. Fish (carp, sturgeon, salmon, and others) is plentiful. Rents are deliberately kept low, as are such costs as public transportation. The government provides free medical and dental care. And if a worker is particularly efficient, he or she may win a free vacation at a government-operated holiday resort.

Soviet planners recognize the need to feed the people adequately. About 40 percent of the Soviet labor force works on the farms and in the forests. (By contrast, only about seven percent of the U.S. labor force does such work.) Nearly all the agricultural land is divided into either state farms, where the workers are paid wages, or collective farms, where the workers are paid lower wages but get a share of the farm's profits.

In good seasons Soviet farmers grow big crops and raise enough cattle and sheep to provide the Soviet people with more than a taste of meat. But crop shortages or failures take place fairly frequently. There are several reasons why.

First, the growing season is short. In much of the Soviet Union there are fewer than a hundred frost-free days a year. Second, a great many Soviet farms are still not completely mechanized. When an early frost looms, all of the crop cannot be harvested by hand — despite the large number of farm workers available. And when there isn't much snow in winter to cover the fields, there may also be a winter wheat crop failure.

Another reason is that each farm family is given a small plot of land for their own use. On it they grow vegetables and raise poultry or livestock — for their consumption or for sale in nearby city markets. When many farmers start neglecting the collective fields in favor of their own, a crop shortage can result.

In recent years, the Soviet Union has made up for its crop shortages by buying abroad. The United States, Canada, and Australia have sold many millions of tons of grain to help feed the Soviet people.

Thus the economic record of the Soviet Union under communism is an uneven one. Few observers can fail to be impressed by the huge industrial plants which have sprung up; the power dams now spanning the rivers; the outstanding Soviet efforts in science, space, medicine; the increases in production. At the same time, Soviet cities are beset by housing shortages. In countless Soviet rural communities, horse-drawn carts sink axle-deep into the mud of unpaved village streets, and the age of indoor plumbing has not yet arrived.

When the world's first Communist state was established in what is now the Soviet Union, its leaders predicted that there would be many hardships. Two generations have sacrificed to build Soviet power. While the people are immensely proud of Soviet accomplishments and the progress that has been made in a little more than a half century, many are also wondering if it isn't about time that more of the country's resources were devoted to making life more comfortable for the people.

*Napoleon's Russian invasion ended in disaster. Moscow
ablaze, the French fled starvation, cold, guerrilla attacks.*

ROAD
TO
REVOLUTION

AS THE 1800'S STARTED, opposition to the system of the
czars was rising. At first, the strongest opposition came
from the nobles who had been educated in Western ideas.
But as the years passed, a new group rose to challenge the
czar. These opponents came from the middle class, people
who were educated, but not necessarily wealthy or powerful. These people — teachers, small businessmen, clerks,
lawyers, doctors, and others — came to hate a system as
backward-looking as that of the czars. And gradually even
the czars and the nobles around them came to realize that
the system was in trouble unless it started making
changes.

The grandson of Catherine II, Czar Alexander I, ruled from 1801 to 1825. He talked about making reforms and actually did make a few, including some plans to abolish serfdom. Alexander is best remembered, however, as the czar who blocked Napoleon's attempt to conquer Russia.

In 1812 Napoleon I, emperor of France, was already master of much of Western Europe. It seemed to him that Russia was ripe for the plucking. So in June of that year, with an army of 600,000, he invaded Russia. The Russians fell back before the French onslaught, but first they destroyed everything in the path of the invaders. Because of the Russians' "scorched-earth" policy, the French army could find little food to seize from Russian farmers.

In September 1812 Napoleon reached Moscow and found it abandoned and in flames. The fire had been set by the last of the retreating Russians and destroyed most of Moscow. Napoleon feared the winds and snow of a subzero Russian winter, so he ordered his troops to retreat. It was a disaster. Plagued by cold, lack of food, and Russian guerrilla attacks, Napoleon saw five of every six of his men killed, captured, or deserted. It was the beginning of the end for the French emperor.

The French threat was ended. But the deeper threat to peace in Russia remained, for many intelligent Russians began to question how long a society could survive in which a tiny group of fabulously wealthy nobles ruled for their own benefit. The ruling class held all the power and almost all the wealth. The peasants — who made up 19 out of every 20 Russians — lived little better than animals.

The first czar who seriously attempted to come to grips with this problem was Alexander II. Alexander was a genuine reformer. In 1861 he freed the serfs. During his reign, he organized banks, built railroads, aided schools, and gave more freedom to the press. He abolished the system that forced many peasants to spend up to 25 years in the army. He even set up limited self-government in small rural communities.

But the freed serfs remained desperately poor. And

they now had to pay for the land they farmed. The gap between the poor (peasants, servants, and factory workers) and the rich (nobles, army officers, and government officials) was enormous. Some Russians wanted more, far more, than Alexander was ready to grant.

Some wanted Russia to become a democratic republic, with a government elected by the people. Some also wanted socialism, with the local or central government running the farms, mines, and factories. Still others wanted anarchism — no central government at all. Peasants occasionally rebelled, and a few middle-class people were involved in plots against the czar. Terrorists tried several times to assassinate Alexander. In 1881 they succeeded.

The attempt of the czars to reform their own system died with Alexander II. The new czar, Alexander III, spent much of his 13 years in power at his country estates while his officials unsuccessfully attemped to break the opposition. Alexander III died in 1894 and his son, Nicholas II, assumed power. He was to be the last czar of Russia.

Nicholas paid little attention to the problems of his people. He believed that he had been chosen by God to rule Russia, and that no mortal power could oppose him. Strikes and protests mounted, but Nicholas was unmoved.

In 1904 Russia went to war with tiny Japan. At the time, almost everyone expected that massive Russia would easily defeat Japan. Instead, Japan inflicted an overwhelming defeat on the poorly trained and ill-equipped Russian army and navy.

A wave of unrest followed the war. On January 22, 1905, the workers of St. Petersburg decided to see the czar personally and perhaps get him to listen to their needs. Unarmed, they assembled before the czar's Winter Palace. Before they could make themselves heard, the czar's soldiers opened fire. Hundreds of workers were killed or wounded.

This "Bloody Sunday" massacre strengthened the people's determination to act. That autumn the workers

In wealth and splendor, Czar Nicholas and wife (above) greet the public. But most Russians were poor, cold, hungry people who had few rights of their own and whose misery is shown on the faces below.

called a general strike. They forced Nicholas to set up an elected parliament. But Nicholas saw this as only a temporary measure to keep the people quiet for a time. Parliament represented the upper classes far more than it did the middle classes, workers, and peasants. Nevertheless, the parliament managed to survive, though without much power, for a decade or so after the Russo-Japanese war.

Then in 1914 World War I began. Russia was plunged into a war with Germany for which it was ill-prepared. On Russia's side were France and Britain, but neither was ready to help Russia directly. Backing Germany were Austria-Hungary and Turkey. For a time it was a seesaw struggle on the Russian front. But by 1916 Russia faced total defeat and utter collapse.

The poorly trained and ill-equipped Russian army was pushed back. It became mutinous. The Russian economy was unable to support the soldiers at the front and the civilians at home. Both soldiers and civilians needed food, fuel, clothing. Most of the people opposed the war and the czar's leadership — or lack of it. Yet Nicholas refused to see what was coming.

In March 1917 the Russian people revolted. This time the revolution was successful. Nicholas was forced to *abdicate* — to give up the throne. A provisional (temporary) government was set up.

Chapter 4

Social Life and Culture

AT FIRST GLANCE, it might seem that a Moslem herdsman from the plains of Soviet central Asia has very little in common with an atheist factory worker in Moscow. Yet foreign visitors to the Soviet Union are sometimes startled at how the various Soviet peoples often seem to think alike. This isn't accidental. More than a half century of education and direction under communism has affected the way the Soviet people think. The Communist government of the Soviet Union has made a deep mark on the daily lives of the Soviet people — regardless of how old they are, what they do, or where they live.

One area of concentrated government control is in the field of education. The Soviet government has made real strides in educating its young people. Most boys and girls attend school six days a week for a total of 10 years. The younger pupils have classes

◄§ It pays to work hard in Soviet schools. Performance in the lower grades determines how far schooling will go.

from 8:30 until noon. The older students go until about 2:30. Then they have youth-group activities in the late afternoon.

It pays to work hard in Soviet schools. Performance in the lower grades determines how far schooling will go. The best students take a stiff examination. If they pass, they receive all-expenses-paid university or professional training from the government. Students usually attend a university for five or six years and from the beginning specialize in one of the sciences or professions, or in business.

The intense Soviet education program has all but wiped out illiteracy in the Soviet Union. As a group, the Soviet people are eager readers. But Soviet authorities view public information as a powerful political tool to mold public opinion in support of government policies. Newspapers, magazines, radio, television, movies, and books all come under the close watch of the censor. Communist Party control of public information is complete — so much so that some Soviet citizens probably aren't even aware of it since they have never known anything else.

The government is everywhere in the Soviet Union — even in sports. The people of the Soviet Union are fond of sports, and most would rather participate than look on. Soccer is the national sport of the Soviet people, with track and field, swimming, skating, skiing, boxing, and wrestling not far behind. The Soviet

Do students take school seriously in the Soviet Union? How much of Soviet progress in science and industrialization is due to basic education?

government also puts great stress on physical fitness, and students in school and workers in factories take part in mass calisthenics.

There are no organized professional sports in the Soviet Union as there are in the U.S. But the Soviet coaches identify young potential star athletes and give them special training. Good athletes are guaranteed an easy, well-paying job, and plenty of time off to train and take part in competition.

Thus, for good or for ill, the Soviet government is deeply involved in almost all aspects of the lives of its citizens. The government has a hand in where people work and where they live. It controls schooling, purchases, communications — even fun and games. Yet Soviet citizens in general do not seem to mind. They are enthusiastic workers, loyal to their country, eager to see it prosper. Life for them is considerably better than it was for their parents or grandparents under the czars. They have had no experience with democracy, and few seem to desire it.

What many Soviet citizens do want, like most people everywhere, is less rigid government controls and more freedom to express themselves. And in the past two decades, the Soviet government has moved somewhat in this direction.

Soviet newspapers now publish letters to the editor complaining about the inefficiency of Soviet society. Soviet writers and artists are now allowed at least a small measure of free expression. But those who go too far in offending the sensibilities of the leadership can expect the massive weight of state criticism to come down on their heads. Still, many Soviet artists and writers continue to fight for individual freedom. They feel that government control curbs artistic creativity.

The people of the Soviet Union have a long tradition of accomplishment in writing and the arts. In the 19th century, few people in Russia could read. Yet Russia produced many talented poets and novelists. Some of them are considered towering giants in literature.

Many critics rank Feodor Dostoyevsky* as the greatest writer of modern times. With profound insight he probed the minds of disturbed people. His stories appeal to people the world over. This is especially true of his novel *Crime and Punishment,* a study of the moral suffering of a murderer.

Dostoyevsky's *The Brothers Karamazov** is another penetrating study of murder. It paints dozens of unforgettable characters in 19th-century Russia. Part of this novel is a "story within a story," called "Christ and the Grand Inquisitor." The Grand Inquisitor asks the question: "Can man bear the burden of freedom?" And he tells Christ that man must be ruled by "miracle, mystery, and authority."

The novels of Count Leo Tolstoy* too stand among the greatest literature. His *War and Peace* is an epic account of Napoleon's invasion and defeat in 1812 (*see* page 47).

Tolstoy was in his prime when he began to question his own aristocratic heritage. He felt that the peasants of Russia, living closer to nature, led healthier lives. He freed his own serfs and worked alongside them. Like the American Henry David Thoreau, Tolstoy spoke out against all violence, especially war.

How could such probing and critical books as those of Tolstoy and Dostoyevsky have been published under the czars? The censors may have believed that they did not endanger a country in which only a small minority could read. Actually there was widespread dissatisfaction with the czarist government among many who could read.

What does today's novelist Solzhenitsyn (left) have in common with 19th-century writers Dostoyevsky (above) and Tolstoy (above right, with wife)? What common threads link the works of modern composer Stravinsky (below) with Soviet love for the movements of classical ballet?

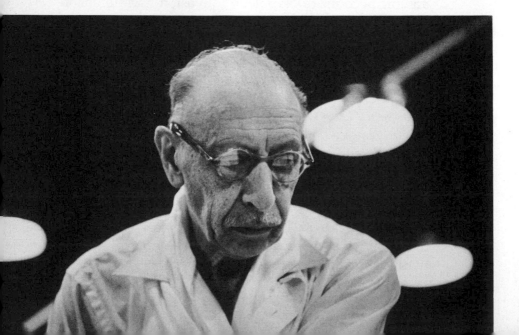

The Soviet Union has a long tradition of accomplishment in writing and the arts.

After Stalin came to power in 1928, a strict control was placed on artists and writers. The government practically dictated what authors wrote. All publishing was a Communist Party monopoly, and all writing had to follow "the Party line." Despite these conditions, some artists managed to create outstanding work. Two recent Soviet authors won Nobel Literature Prizes, but displeased their government and were made to suffer for it.

Boris Pasternak* was forced to have the manuscript of his book *Dr. Zhivago** smuggled out of the Soviet Union because Soviet authorities refused to publish it. Yet it won the 1958 Nobel Prize. However, Pasternak was denied permission to go to Sweden to accept the award, and so had to reject it.

Alexander Solzhenitsyn* won the Nobel Prize for Literature in 1970. He was warned that if he left the Soviet Union to receive the prize he might not be allowed to return. Finally the award was presented to him in a private ceremony in Moscow. He remained under a cloud because he continued to write novels that were in part critical of the Soviet government.

Other modern Soviet writers have been jailed or confined to mental hospitals for voicing their discontent. Some of them continue to speak out whenever they can, and thus keep alive the spark of individual freedom.

Both under the czars and the Communists, some of the world's greatest musicians have been Russians. Perhaps best known of the Russian composers is Peter Ilyich Tchaikovsky,* who lived in the last half of the 19th century. His symphonies and operas, and his ballets, *Swan Lake*, *Sleeping Beauty*, and *Nutcracker,* are the best known.

Igor Stravinsky* was a great pioneer of modern

music. He was born in Russia, moved to France, and then became an American citizen. He died in New York in 1972. His famous *The Rite of Spring* is a stirring and colorful composition. His ballets, *The Firebird* and *Petrouchka*,* are based on old Russian folk tales.

Of all the arts in the Soviet Union, the most popular is ballet. The Soviet people follow it closely and enthusiastically. More than two centuries ago, the children of serfs were taught dancing in St. Petersburg in order to perform for the czars. Thus began what is today known as the Leningrad Ballet. A still more famous troupe, the Bolshoi,* has more than 2,500 dancers and often tours the U.S.

☆　☆　☆　☆　☆　☆　☆　☆　☆

Since the death of dictator Joseph Stalin (*see* page 70) in 1953, the government has gone through periods when it allowed more artistic freedom and periods when it clamped back down on artists who strayed from "the Party line." Today Soviet society is seeking a new balance between state authority and individual liberty. Where once there was no freedom to criticize, today there is some. But how far can the government go in allowing criticism before its very authority is challenged? Will greater relaxation of controls bring even more pressure for individual freedom?

*This historic photograph shows the Bolsheviks storming
the Leningrad Winter Palace and taking over government.*

THE
RUSSIAN
REVOLUTION

THE REVOLUTION OF MARCH 1917 was not a Communist
revolution at first. Rather, it was an uprising by peasants,
workers, and soldiers which had little plan or leadership.
On their own, peasants seized many estates. Workers took
over mines and factories. Soldiers left the front lines of
the war against Germany and started walking home.

Out of this chaos, two power blocs emerged. One was
the provisional government. The other was called the
Soviet (council) of Workers' and Soldiers' Deputies. Soon

this council was demanding more than the provisional government could provide. In particular, it wanted Russia to withdraw from World War I. It believed that only one man was strong enough to lead Russia out of the war. That man was V. I. Lenin.*

In April 1917 Lenin returned to Russia. For 10 years he had been in exile, most recently in Switzerland. Now he appeared in Petrograd.* (This was the new name for the city of St. Petersburg. It had been changed at the outbreak of World War I because the old name sounded too German.) Yet it was actually the German government which had helped get Lenin back into Russia. The Germans hoped that his presence would increase the pressure on the provisional government to drop out of the fighting.

Lenin was a dynamic, intense leader. Born in 1870, his real name was Vladimir Illich Ulyanov.* He was 17 when his older brother, Alexander, was arrested for plotting to murder the czar. Alexander Ulyanov and four other students were executed. This action embittered young Vladimir. It made him hate all people of wealth and property, and it led him to join the movement to overthrow the czarist system.

After practicing law for a time, Vladimir joined the underground revolutionary movement. In 1895 he was arrested. Imprisoned for 14 months, he was later sent to exile in Siberia. There he adopted the name of Lenin, perhaps after Siberia's Lena River, and married a woman who had also been sent to Siberia. This was the period when Lenin developed his political ideas.

After three years in Siberia, the Lenins were released, and were able to travel outside Russia. They went from country to country in Western Europe, editing a Marxist paper called The Spark, which was smuggled back into Russia. About then the Marxists split into two sections — the Bolsheviks* and the Mensheviks.* Lenin, who was still in exile, took command of the Bolshevik section. He taught the Bolsheviks many revolutionary tactics.

A month after Lenin returned to Petrograd, he was

joined by Leon Trotsky. Trotsky was another fiery revolutionary who also had been in exile for a long time. Lenin and Trotsky made a powerful team.

At once Lenin and his Bolsheviks broke with the provisional government. Lenin demanded an immediate peace with Germany. But Alexander Kerensky,* the provisional government leader, was under pressure from Britain and the United States to keep on fighting. Kerensky, whose government had many democratic features, launched a new attack against the Germans. But his forces were badly beaten. He had to face riots and demonstrations in Petrograd. And he had to deal with power-hungry groups in the army. Kerensky was in real trouble.

Then Lenin made his move. On November 7, 1917, the Bolsheviks stormed the winter palace where the provisional government was sitting. At gun-point they threw out Kerensky's government and took over. Lenin made two proclamations. One was a call to all warring nations to make peace. The other was to abolish private property in Russia and to seize all land — moves that were basic to communism. The slogan of the revolutionary government was "Bread, Land, and Peace."

The new government left the Allies and signed a separate peace treaty with Germany in March 1918. Then it moved to crush all opposition. Czar Nicholas II and his family had been imprisoned since the czar's abdication in March 1917. One night they were taken into a cellar by their Bolshevik guards and executed. Other opponents were imprisoned or executed.

The capital was moved from Petrograd to Moscow, and the Bolsheviks organized their own Red Army. The Red Army was soon involved in a long struggle with anti-Communist forces inside Russia. These forces, called the Whites, were led largely by the old upper classes. They were aided by the United States, France, Britain, Japan, and other nations opposed to communism. But the Whites were poorly organized, and foreign aid was not enough to sustain them. By 1920 the White forces were largely wiped out — the Communists controlled all of Russia.

But the war, the revolution, and the civil war had drained Russia's resources, both human and natural. Millions of soldiers and civilians had been killed or had died of disease. Countless others had fled the country.

The Union of Soviet Socialist Republics was established in 1922. (Over the next 18 years the number of republics grew from four to 15.) That same year Lenin fell seriously ill. He died two years later.

Today Lenin is revered almost as a saint in the Soviet Union. Petrograd has been renamed Leningrad. Lenin's embalmed body remains on view in Red Square, and thousands of Soviet citizens file by it every day. They feel that without Lenin the 1917 Revolution and the creation of the Soviet government would have been impossible.

Lenin: Was he villain or hero? How will history view this man who led forces that established communism in Russia?

2
LIFE IN THE SOVIET UNION

Chapter 5

East of the Urals

PICNICS IN THE WILD GRASS along the Bratsk* Sea end early in the evening, for it gets cold when the sun sets. Dmitri,* who is 13, his 15-year-old sister, Kira,* and their parents come here often in the summer. They build a fire and have supper — a thick fish soup, pickles, some raw onions, black bread, and plums. Kira often goes into the forest to pick large flowers that look like tulips. Dmitri hunts for bugs.

The Bratsk Sea is not a sea, but a large lake in Soviet Siberia. It is man-made and very new. Its waters were dammed from the Angara* River to furnish power for a huge hydroelectric plant.

The city of Bratsk, where the family of Dmitri and Kira lives, began to grow around the power plant in the mid-1950's. Since then engineers and their families from all parts of the Soviet Union have come to help run the plant. To serve the new settlement, teachers, doctors, storekeepers, seamstresses, and

✍ The city of Bratsk began to grow around the power plant in the 1950's. Since then engineers and their families from all parts of the Soviet Union have come to help run the plant.

---

builders have come too. Together they have made Bratsk one of the largest and busiest of Siberia's "new" cities.

Dmitri's parents, Grigory* and Elina,* were born in the warm Soviet republic of Georgia. The move to Siberia was like that of an American moving from Florida to the Arctic Circle. In parts of Siberia, winter lasts for 10 long months. Temperatures drop as low as -94°F.

Not too long ago, most of what is today Bratsk was thick forest. It had to be cut away before Bratsk could be built. So today most of the settled land here has no trees. In summer the ground cracks and dries, and covers everything with a thick coat of dust. Only a few streets are paved.

If life is so hard and lonely here, why do people come? "Salaries and housing allowances are good," says Grigory, an engineer at the power plant. "Siberia's resources are only beginning to be tapped. They say that more than half of the world's coal and oil are under the ground here. There's natural gas and timber too. And the government financed our move from Tbilisi* [Georgia's capital]."

Elina works at a cellulose plant in Bratsk. "The cost of living is no higher than anywhere else in the Soviet Union. But I earn a third more here than I did in Georgia. That means more clothes for the family, better food, and maybe one day a car. We like the chance to build a new life for ourselves."

66

The Bratsk hydroelectric station, deep in the Siberian wilderness, generates power for many Soviet industries and homes. Siberia's power potential was one strong reason for setting up communities in this icebound, isolated land.

Dmitri also likes the adventure of living in Bratsk. He wants to be a geologist, so Siberia is a good place for him. On camping trips, he prospects for gold, uranium, diamonds, nickel, and zinc. Every time he finds something unusual, he labels it and gives it to his expedition leader, an expert geologist.

"For many of my friends, coming to Siberia was like entering a contest," says Kira. "This is because they had to compete with many other students for admission to the Mathematics-Physics School."

Kira's school, serving grades nine and 10, is for good students. Students attend 30 hours of classes a week, concentrating on math and physics. There are also optional lectures, seminars, laboratory and practical work in art, photography, theater, poetry,

All over Siberia today, modern cities are spring-
ing out of barren wilderness to tap land's wealth:
timber, minerals, and water power for electricity.

typing, shorthand, mechanical drawing, and nuclear physics.

Kira hopes to go to the university. With her 4.5 average (out of a possible 5.0) at the school, and a membership in Komsomol,* her admission — plus a generous living allowance — is almost guaranteed. Komsomol is a voluntary organization for young people 15 to 27 years old. It is sponsored by the Communist Party. Nearly half the Soviet young people in that age group belong.

Membership in Komsomol means hard work. In summers the members help plow fields, build houses, string telephone lines. During the school year they rally voters to the polls, act as marshals at parades, and do other kinds of community service. And they are expected to attend regular after-school lectures about communism.

"I don't go to too many Komsomol lectures," admits Kira. "And my group leader has criticized me for it. But I have four or five hours of homework every night. Whenever I have a little spare time, I like to go to the Eureka.*"

The Eureka is a Komsomol-operated café. It is so popular that patrons must sometimes wait in line for an hour or more for a table and a chance to hear the live music.

"You've got to be 18 or older to get in," says Kira. "But I help out with refreshments on Friday nights, so I get to hear the music. Last week I heard the Loud Group. They had three guitar players and a drummer. They played some old Beatle songs and 'When the Saints Go Marching In!' "

Komsomol is at the center of school life. It arranges student trips to other cities in Siberia. It organizes young people's dances on Saturday nights. It plans sports contests. It also gives some students a chance to visit other countries at government expense.

Why wasn't Siberia settled by European Russians sooner? For one reason, the Siberian natives were hostile. For another, the cold climate and deep forests prevented any kind of large-scale farming until the late 1950's. In fact, before then the only people who came to Siberia in great numbers were those sent to forced labor camps during the 1930's and 1940's (see page 72). And it was only after those laborers began to develop Siberia's oil and natural gas deposits that it became a more livable area.

*Smiling Stalin was cruel despot. Behind Stalin is aide,
Nikita Khrushchev, who also became dictator of Soviet Union.*

STALIN AND AFTER

EVEN BEFORE LENIN'S DEATH, a power struggle for his
post was taking place. The leading contenders were Leon
Trotsky and Joseph Stalin, a long-time Bolshevik leader.

Stalin's real name was Djugashvili.* He adopted the
alias of Stalin, meaning "steel," when he escaped from a
czarist prison in 1912. Born in 1879 in the province of

Georgia in the Caucasian Mountains, Stalin was the son of a shoemaker. As a teen-ager he wanted to be a priest and actually began studying for the priesthood. However, he soon became more interested in politics than religion, and turned to communism.

At secret meetings of the Bolsheviks, Stalin won Lenin's notice. Lenin made him a member of the Bolshevik inner circle in 1912. Stalin was arrested again in 1913 and was not released until Alexander Kerensky freed all political prisoners after the czar's fall in 1917.

Stalin's climb to power took place after his release from prison. He served as a lower-rung official for five years. In 1922 he was appointed General Secretary of the Communist Party, second in power only to Lenin.

But even Lenin in his last days distrusted Stalin. He wrote, "Stalin is too rough." After Lenin's death, Stalin forced Trotsky to resign as war minister. Later he expelled Trotsky from the Party and sent him into exile. (Trotsky eventually went to Mexico, where he was murdered in 1940. Stalin is generally believed to have ordered the slaying.)

With Lenin dead and Trotsky in exile, Stalin was master of the Soviet Union. He was a cruel and cunning dictator. Stalin realized that the U.S.S.R. was decades behind the Western nations in production and national defense. If the lag was not made up soon, he reasoned, his country would be taken over by more advanced nations bent on conquest. So he pushed the Soviet Union hard.

In 1928 Stalin launched the first of a series of Five-Year Plans. These were designed to make the U.S.S.R. economically and militarily strong. At that time many farmers worked their own land. He forced them to group their plots of land into huge collective or state farms. The farmers who resisted were murdered. He concentrated on heavy, or basic, industries, and forgot that the people had their own basic needs of food, clothing, and housing.

As time passed, Stalin grew even more ruthless. In 1934 he began a "purge" of opposition in the Party and Red

Army. He charged that hundreds of high-ranking Party members and top army officers were "plotting against the state," and had them put to death. Millions more were arrested and sent to forced labor camps.

All this happened in the 1930's, a time when Nazi dictator Adolf Hitler was in power in Germany. The Nazis and the Communists were sworn enemies. Yet in the days just before the beginning of World War II, Stalin signed a treaty with Hitler's Germany. The pact actually meant that each nation could invade and take over territories without opposition from the other. The war started on September 1, 1939, when Germany invaded Poland from the west. Soon the Soviet Union invaded Poland from the east, claiming that it was only trying to protect its own borders.

Within a year the U.S.S.R. had also seized a chunk of Finland; the independent Baltic nations of Estonia, Latvia, and Lithuania (see page 30); and parts of Rumania called Bessarabia* and northern Bucovina. All were made a part of the Soviet Union.

But in June 1941 Germany suddenly turned on its Soviet ally. The Nazis invaded the Soviet Union with troops, tanks, and planes, driving to the outskirts of Moscow and Leningrad. The Soviet Union then joined the Western Allies as a partner in the war. The U.S. in particular supplied the Soviet Union with huge quantities of munitions, food, and fuel.

Soviet troops drove the Germans from Moscow's steps in early 1942. During the savage winter of 1942-43, the Red Army encircled the Germans at Stalingrad (see page 92). But the German siege of Leningrad hung on until January 1944. Then the Nazis were driven back.

Beginning in the summer of 1944 the Soviet armies advanced steadily westward. They pushed across the Nazi-held countries of Eastern Europe and into Eastern Germany. Meanwhile the Western Allies were advancing across France and Western Germany. By April 1945 Soviet troops were in Berlin, Germany's capital. Germany surrendered on May 7.

World War II had taken a terrible toll in Soviet lives and property. Soviet losses were far greater than any other country in the war, including defeated Germany. Soviet military casualties numbered about 7.5 million. And there were probably about two Soviet civilian casualties for each military one. Vast areas lay in ruins.

Yet after the war the Soviet Union did more than concentrate on rebuilding its own country. It turned the eastern zone of Germany, which it had occupied right after the war, into a Communist state. It did the same to the other East European countries once held by the Nazis, making them satellites around itself as planet. For years after the war, planet and satellites were involved in a Cold War against the West.

Stalin died in 1953, and Nikita S. Khrushchev* became the boss of the U.S.S.R. He too was a dictator. But he was more generous to the Soviet people. And he openly accused Stalin of poor leadership and even mass murder.

Khrushchev tried to ease the Cold War by announcing a policy of what he called "peaceful coexistence." He said the Soviet Union would compete with other countries in industry and science, not in war. As one step in science competition, the Soviets in 1957 launched Sputnik I, the first spacecraft to circle the earth. It was a long time before the United States was able to catch up with the U.S.S.R. in space achievements.

Gradually through the 1960's relations between the U.S. and the Soviet Union improved. But there were setbacks. For instance, in 1962 the Soviet Union installed missile-launching sites in Communist Cuba. The United States soon learned of these and ringed Cuba with a naval blockade to prevent delivery of more missiles. In a tense confrontation, U.S. President John F. Kennedy demanded that Khrushchev remove all missiles and sites. Khrushchev did so.

But by the early 1970's relations had improved so much that President Richard Nixon was able to exchange visits with Leonid Brezhnev,* Communist Party chief. Their talks set up new understandings between the U.S. and the

U.S.S.R. More trade, more exchanges of scientific and technical data, and more swaps of artistic works and performers were only part of the agreements reached.

While the Soviet Union's relations with the West were improving, its relations with the People's Republic of China (Communist China) were deteriorating. China had been friendly with the Soviet Union after the Chinese Communist take-over in 1949. But the two giants — the Soviet Union, the world's biggest in area; China, the world's biggest in population — soon disagreed on many matters.

They argued about how communism should best be carried out. They quarreled over boundaries between the two countries. They quit sharing nuclear research data. Ancient hostilities came to the surface.

Today the Soviet Union still believes that communism is the best kind of government and economic system. However, it now limits its use of force in trying to spread communism. At present, it is not willing to risk open war in order to further the spread of communism.

In the Cold War days of 1960's, a display of Soviet military might was intended to impress other nations.

Chapter 6

Moscow: Nerve Center

YURI* MAKES HIMSELF DO sit-up exercises every morning when the alarm goes off at seven. But even after breakfast he doesn't begin to wake up until he gets on the bus for school. Most of the other students on the bus are too sleepy to make much noise. They ride quietly and watch the city of Moscow wake up.

Because he was named after its founder, Yuri is proud of living in Moscow. In the 1100's Prince Yuri Dolgoruky* seized the forest, which was to become the site of the city, by drowning its owner in a pond. The prince then built a wooden fort and trading post on the land and named it Moscow, meaning "troubled waters." Today Moscow is a city of seven million people, capital and "nerve center" of the Soviet Union.

Today more and more Moscow families are moving into new housing. Most of the new buildings provide a family of four with a living room, two small bedrooms, a bathroom, and a kitchen. But the waiting list for new quarters is still very long. The government, which owns all houses of more than six rooms and all apartment buildings, maintains the list.

In getting a new apartment, it helps to be a member of the Communist Party. Only about five percent of the people in the Soviet Union belong to the Party. These people are the elite, for the Communist Party is the only political party permitted to exist in the Soviet Union.

Yuri's father and mother are Party members. They attend regular meetings of their local Party branch. Sometimes, Yuri's mother admits, the meetings are long and boring. But the Party speaks for the government, and the government controls the land, the waters, the resources, all means of production, transportation, communication, virtually all housing, and so on and so on. So Yuri's mother forces herself to pay attention at the meetings.

Yuri's grandmother, who lives with the family, cannot be bothered with Party membership. She is a religious woman. And the Party says that churchgoers are not good citizens, for they think more about God than about Lenin.

Both of Yuri's parents work, so the grandmother keeps house. She cooks the meals on the two-burner stove. Since she has no refrigerator, she puts spoilable food on a window ledge. And she does most of her food shopping at a neighborhood *gastronom*.* There she buys potatoes, cabbage, onions, beets, other vegetables. She must go to another store for meat, to a third one for bread and cake, and to a fourth for milk, cheese, and eggs.

A new apartment house looms over an ancient building that was once a Russian Orthodox church.

At each gastronom she spends a lot of time waiting in line. First she puts her purchases on a counter where the price is totaled. Next she pays a cashier and gets a receipt. Finally she hands the receipt to a wrapper, who records the sale before releasing the merchandise. It is a slow process.

American-style supermarkets are rare in the Soviet Union. More typical is a shop such as the Central Market on Tsvetanoi* Boulevard. It displays produce from all over the Soviet Union. Farmers come by truck and train to sell what they've raised themselves on their small backyard plots.

Today private backyard gardens supply the nation with much of its total farm needs, even though they make up only three percent of the cultivated land of the Soviet Union. Farmers make three or four week-long trips a year to the Central Market, and set their own prices. Buyers don't object to paying more, for the quality is much better than at the goverment stores.

The fastest way to get from central Moscow to Yuri's house is on the Metro, or subway. The walls of most of the Metro's stations are decorated with colorful tiles and paintings. Some stations have statues set in arched nooks. The cost of a ride is five kopeks* (about seven U.S. cents.)

Public transportation is good. Marina,* Yuri's older sister, jokes that this is because women helped build the subways and even drive the buses. Yuri answers that he would feel much safer if fewer women did men's work. Marina then reminds Yuri of the photo on his wall: It shows Valentina Tereshkova,* the first woman to fly in space. "Aren't you proud of her?" she asks.

On snowy, blowy days in Moscow, Marina often goes to the Lenin Hills for a view of the city and a

⇥ At each store, people spend a lot of time waiting in line.

---

fast ski run down the slopes. The view is something like the one Napoleon Bonaparte had when he led his French army to the edge of Moscow in 1812 (*see* page 47).

Marina sometimes goes skiing with her university friends near Napoleon's camp grounds. From a point near the first flag of the slalom run, a skier can see St. Basil's and the Kremlin* (*see* page 84) — and rows of new apartment buildings spreading out on both sides of Lenin Stadium.

Many buildings of the Moscow State University are located in these Lenin Hills. Tall and towered, the buildings are typical of the massive structures built in Stalin's time. People joke that they look like wedding cakes.

The university is large, with about 35,000 students enrolled. Nearly half attend evening school or take correspondence courses. It's possible to live at the university for months without going beyond its walls. There are shops and stores of all kinds, restaurants and cafeterias, and a gym, swimming pool, and beauty parlor.

Until last year, Marina spent many Saturday evenings in one of the dormitories. Her boyfriend, Grisha,* lived there until he finished his university studies and won a fellowship to study in Leningrad.

Grisha and his roommate shared a two-room suite in the dormitory. On Saturday nights they would invite friends over. The small room in which they gathered was furnished with a bookcase, a table, an Oriental rug, and a daybed. Even three people made a crowd in the room.

At Moscow's GUM department store, customers wait. Since the demand from Soviet consumers often exceeds the supply, the result is usually a long line.

But there were always at least six in the room on Saturday nights. They would talk, tell jokes, and listen to taped music. (Records are expensive in the U.S.S.R. and are usually classics. Most new music is taped from Western radio broadcasts.)

Sometimes Marina and Grisha went to the theater. Tickets are inexpensive by American standards, mainly because the Soviet government pays the cost of most theater productions. But the government also reserves the right to censor what is said and shown onstage.

On the day before Grisha left for Leningrad last year, he and Marina went to the theater. Afterward Grisha talked about getting married. Marina expects

**∽§ On signal all come together
and line up, two by two, with the
bride and groom leading.**

the topic will come up again when she visits Grisha in Leningrad next summer.

Marina has already imagined some details of her own wedding. For example, it would take place at the Marriage Palace in Moscow. She would wear a short white gown — she saw a pretty one recently for 45 rubles (about $56). She and Grisha would pick out his wedding suit and perhaps some china, linen, and other household goods at one of Moscow's wedding shops. They would each invite about a dozen friends to the ceremony. Afterward their parents would prepare a family celebration when the couple finally returned home.

The wedding ceremony would follow an officially approved pattern. When the group enters the Marriage Palace, the bride and her friends are shown to one waiting room, the groom and his friends to another. On signal all come together in the corridor and line up, two by two, with the bride and groom leading. Then, to a wedding march played over a loudspeaker, the procession moves into the main room.

There, standing on thick carpeting beneath elegant chandeliers, the party gathers around three desks presided over by wedding officials. One official records the couple's names and the date of their marriage. Another asks them if it is their "sincere desire" to wed. The third gives them a short speech of formal congratulations. The bride and groom then kiss, sign a register, and lead their friends out of the room as the loudspeaker plays a waltz tune.

Marina can't wait for the day. But she tells herself that she musn't think too much about it — at least not until she has seen Grisha again.

At Moscow's Marriage Palace, a happy young
couple and attendants begin wedding procession.

The ancient walls and towers of the Kremlin, seat of Soviet power, watch over Moscow like a giant guarding the city.

THE
KREMLIN

KREMLIN IN RUSSIAN means "fortress." Moscow's Kremlin stands where Prince Yuri built his wooden fort in the 12th century. For several decades, Moscow expanded slowly. Then, in the early 13th century, the Mongols, or Tatars, under a grandson of Genghis Khan, swept out of Asia and overran much of southern and central Russia, including Moscow. The town was burned at least a half-dozen times by the Tatars.

Still, Moscow survived, and even began to grow. It was aided by its central position on the Moscow River, which gave it access to many of the major rivers of central Russia, including the Volga, Don, and Dneiper.

A later ruler of Moscow married a sister of one of the Tatar rulers. This helped boost the prestige of the city. Even further prestige came when, in the early part of the 14th century, Moscow became the home of the chief bishop, or Metropolitan, of Russia. When Constantinople, which had been the center of the Orthodox Church, was captured by the Moslem Turks in 1453, Moscow became the eastern headquarters of the Church.

The first great Kremlin tower was built by Ivan III in 1485 to help prevent another Tatar attack. It is called the Secret Tower because it has a hiding place inside of which a person could be concealed in time of siege.

Ivan III was a highly independent leader. He was the first Russian prince to refuse to pay taxes to the Tatars. In 1480, after a series of battles, he rid his country completely of Tatar rule. And he expanded the borders of Moscow to take in the nearby ancient city of Novgorod. His people were so proud of their leader that they nicknamed him "Ivan the Great."

Later czars expanded and improved the Kremlin many times, erecting palaces, churches, and government buildings. St. Basil's Cathedral, for example, was built by another Ivan — Ivan the Terrible — to commemorate his victory over the Tatars in 1552. The victory destroyed Mongol power in Russia.

There was no room within the Kremlin walls for St. Basil's Cathedral. So Ivan had it built just outside the walls, in what is now known as Red Square. Today the cathedral is a museum, not a church. The gold tips on its many-spiraled domes remind visitors of the riches of the czars.

But the Kremlin today does more than remind people of the czarist age. The Kremlin is also the administrative center of the Soviet Union. It spreads out in a giant triangle over 65 acres of Moscow, its rose-colored walls alive with towers and turrets. Right outside the Kremlin is Red Square, famous for its parades displaying Soviet military might. The tomb of the Soviet Union's greatest hero, Lenin, stands in this square.

Ancient Russian print shows the Battle of Kulikovo in 1380 at which the Russians, right, defeated the Tatars.

Chapter 7

"Mother Volga Is Russia"

THE VOLGA is the most important transport river in the Soviet Union. Its waters, still and shallow compared to other Russian rivers, stretch like a winding ribbon from a point near Leningrad to a delta on the Caspian Sea (*see* map on page 29). Stringlike tributaries feed into it in many places along the way. It is a transport route for one half of all the Soviet Union's freight. It carries timber and manufactured goods to the south. It carries oil, grain, meat, and fish to the north. Its basin serves as a home for more than a fourth of the Soviet people. Its dams furnish electricity for homes and industries.

But the Volga is changing fast as new towns grow up along it. Each time a new dam is built on the river to serve people and industry, a man-made lake is created. Each time a new canal is dug, several more man-made lakes come into being. The lakes are "spill-offs," controlled by more dikes and dams.

Some Soviet ecologists say that the Volga will soon have so many dams and reservoirs and canals added to it that it will cease to be a real river. It will become only a lifeless strip of controlled water.

The ecologists also point out that too little of the Volga is being permitted to flow into the Caspian Sea. The sea, they say, is shrinking. Its fish — such as the sturgeon whose eggs provide some of the world's best and most expensive black caviar — are threatened.

"*Matushka** Volga, Mother Volga, *is* Russia," is an old Russian saying. Tanya* agrees. "The river is our heritage and a great part of our history. It will not disappear, no matter what we do."

Tanya, 16, and her boyfriend, Sasha,* 17, are sitting on a beach of yellow sand across the river from the city of Volgograd.* It is early July. The temperature is 69 degrees, and it is almost dusk. The day has been like most July days around Volgograd — it sped by swiftly and pleasantly.

Only the young people stay at the beach when the sun goes down. They build campfires and stretch out on their beach blankets. Someone has a guitar. Someone else tries to read a book by the firelight. A third person shivers near the fire, drying his wet pants-legs and frying some freshly caught *ukha,** the troutlike fish of the Volga. Everyone is having a good time. They sing old Russian songs as they eat the fish and drink *kvas,** a popular fermented-bread drink. And many soon doze off under the star-speckled sky.

Volgograd is 500 miles southeast of Moscow. To the east of the city are the deserts of the Kazakh* Republic. To the west is the Tsimlyansk* Sea, a man-made lake formed as a by-product of the canal linking the Volga and Don rivers. The land around the

An outdoor bookstall in Volgograd. What was Volgograd's former name? Why the name change?

city is dry and flat. Only the electric-light poles connecting the city to the dam break up the landscape.

Volgograd's original name was Tsaritsyn,* a Tatar word meaning "yellow sands along the yellow river." In 1924, when Joseph Stalin came to power, Tsaritsyn became Stalingrad.

It was here along the lower Volga that a five-month battle in 1942 helped turn the tide against the Nazis in World War II (see page 92). People came back slowly to Stalingrad after World War II. Homeless in the ruined city, they built log cabins just like those of their peasant ancestors. Some of the cabins remain today, but most of the city looks new.

North of the city proper is a gigantic monument commemorating the Battle of Stalingrad. The monument, called "Motherland," is a statue of a woman that stands 18 feet tall. The woman holds a sword

89

✑ Some Soviet ecologists say that the Volga will soon have so many dams and canals that it will cease to be a real river.

high above her head. Below her are smaller statues of heroic-looking soldiers and civilians, with fountains around them.

Before Motherland was erected, the city had another famous sculpture. This was a huge statue of Joseph Stalin, which towered over the central square. It was abruptly removed in 1961 by order of Nikita Khrushchev, the Communist Party leader. And the city's name was changed a third time, to Volgograd.

Khrushchev had taken over power some time after Stalin's death in 1953. He then accused Stalin of cruelty and of many crimes against the state. He said that the Soviet people had been wrong to "worship" one man. And he ordered the renaming of all towns, streets, schools, factories, and so on that had been named after Stalin. At the end of several years of "de-Stalinization," only one well-known street remained to honor the dead Party chief: Stalin Boulevard in Gori, Georgia, where he was born.

In spite of the constant changes along the Volga, there is much that stays the same. There are still little villages where the men wear blousy tunics and floppy trousers tucked into boots. The cottages have electric lights, but water must be pumped from an outdoor well. People's lives revolve around the farm and the village marketplace. New ways, already well established in the cities and larger towns, seep down only slowly to these villages. And the river is the only road to the world beyond.

The Volga, great water road through the Soviet Union, is alive with traffic and construction.

Soviet soldiers and civilians fought for their city and their lives in World War II's epic Battle of Stalingrad.

THE BATTLE
OF
STALINGRAD

A MILITARY HISTORIAN named David Eggenberger calls the battle of Stalingrad "one of the decisive battles of World War II and one of the great turning points in military history."

Why was this battle between the Nazi German forces and the army of the Soviet Union so important? The main reason is that it stopped the Nazi march eastward to Soviet oil and coal fields and good farmlands. It was the first major step in the final defeat of Nazi dictator Adolf Hitler.

At first the German attack on Stalingrad promised to be another triumph. In August 1942 German ground forces reached the city's western outskirts and began their assault on the central city. They were opposed by a Soviet army, helped by civilians, that made the Germans pay heavily for every street and square block they took.

But by September the Nazis had fought their way to the center of Stalingrad. They found it pounded to rubble by their artillery fire. Some Soviet forces had retreated east across the Volga, and others were holed up north and south of the city. They were waiting for winter.

In November the severe cold came, and the Soviets launched their own counterattack. From their positions north and south of Stalingrad they moved west, routing one vast Nazi force and encircling another, the whole German Sixth Army. The Sixth was trapped in a ring of steel 25 miles in diameter.

Winter weather, strong Soviet defenses, and lack of equipment kept the German air force from supplying the 300,000 Nazi troops adequately. The Soviets defeated all attempts to break through the ring. Nazi troops were ordered to fight to the last man.

In January 1943 the Soviets began tightening the ring. When Hitler refused to let the Sixth Army surrender, Soviet tanks and artillery moved in for the kill. In a month it was all over. Only 91,000 of the original 300,000 Nazi troops remained alive. The Nazi drive to the east was halted, and the Soviet thrust to the west had begun. It would end two years later with the Soviets marching into Berlin.

THE LAND

*The Soviet land is vaster and more
varied than almost any other nation's
on earth. In the south near the
Black Sea (left), the land is lush
and green. In sharp contrast is
the treeless but fertile steppe west
of the Ural Mountain range (below).*

*VARIETY: Eastern Europe is a land of swift
rivers like the Danube (above); squat mountains,
as in Yugoslavia (above right); and rolling
plains, as in Rumania (right). The land is
lovely, but it often yields only a meager living.*

CITIES: Is there a link between the man-made city and the national culture which nursed it? Rebuilt East Berlin (above), an old Yugoslav town (below), and Moscow's Kremlin Museum each in its own way reflects its culture and values.

98

THE PEOPLE

In the Communist world, the government is important in people's lives. This woman (left) carrying a pennant which says "To the Cosmonauts, Glory!" proudly wears government medals for farming achievements. Sculptors (below) use their talents to create art exalting communism.

INDIVIDUALS: The people of so vast an area
as is covered in this book can't be summed up
in a few pat phrases. They are all individuals.
Above, a group of Polish youths; below, Rumanian
workers; right, an elderly person in Leningrad
in the Soviet Union. You be the caption-writer.
In a few sentences, you describe each photograph.

PASTIMES: *Work, as in an Albanian factory (below left) or on the snowy wastes of Soviet central Asia (right), gives meaning to people's lives. So does leisure, as on a Soviet volleyball court (left) or in Yugoslav bazaar (below).*

THE ECONOMY

Once agriculture, as on the Rumanian collective farm (below), was the chief economic activity in the Soviet Union and Eastern Europe. Now such industries as the Soviet steel mill (left) are becoming more important. Farms are being mechanized; factories are being computerized.

PEOPLE: *Whether Communist, capitalist, or
something in between, an economy is molded
by the economic activities of its people.
What do the pictures on pages 106-111 tell
you about economic life in a Communist state?*

108

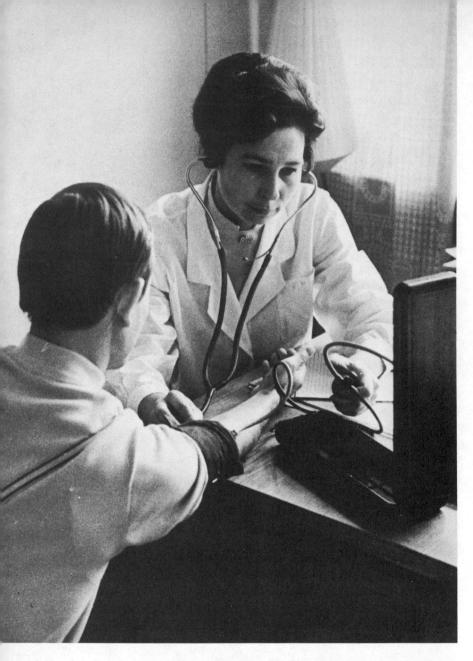

CONTROL: *The Communist states described
in this book make most economic decisions,
provide many services, but allow some
private enterprise. A worker gets a free medical
examination in the Soviet Union (above);
a Yugoslav boy sells peaches along the road
(above right); Rumanian factory appren-
tices in a state-run dining room (right).*

110

THE CULTURE

Traditions and folkways — the culture of a people — may be stronger than politics. The Russian Orthodox Church (at left a ceremony), though hampered by the state, is not dead. The Polish Easter custom of donning national dress and being splashed with water, which began in pre-Christian days, is still observed.

HERITAGE: The Soviet people today are heirs of Old Russia's rich artistic heritage. Above, elaborate onion-shaped domes of Moscow's St. Basil's Cathedral; above right, Mother and Child ikon* which decorated a church; right, carved wooden lion which decorated a home.

CRAFTS: *A people's traditions emerge from a study of their arts and crafts. The Czech goblet, the Russian carved rooster, the Rumanian embroidery, and the Polish tapestry all show the practiced and careful hand of the craftsperson.*

3
THE
BALKANS

Chapter 8

Bulgaria Depends on Uncle Ivan

FOUR COUNTRIES make up the area known as the Balkans. They are Albania, Bulgaria, Rumania, and Yugoslavia. (Greece is sometimes considered a Balkan nation, but as its system of government is different from the other Balkan nations, it is not treated in this book.) Each of these nations has its own language or languages and its own ancient origins, loyalties, and traditions. At times in the past, the peoples of the Balkans have been united against a common foe. But more often they have been divided by ancient differences.

Still, the Balkan nations have some things in common. One of these is their system of government. Each of the four nations is Communistic, although the brand of communism in each nation is different. Also, the nations are closely intertwined in a history of wars, hostilities, and upheavals, which at one time made the name "Balkan" a code word for turbu-

119

lence. Thus it is logical to consider these nations as a unit in the study of the Soviet Union and Eastern Europe.

☆ ☆ ☆ ☆ ☆ ☆ ☆ ☆ ☆

Leading the best-seller list in Sofia,* Bulgaria's capital, a while back, was a novel called *Avakoum Zahov* Against 07*. Avakoum Zahov, the hero, is a secret agent of the Bulgarian Communist government. His mission is to keep a dread death ray from falling into the hands of 07, an agent from the West. The two have a showdown on an Antarctic glacier. Zahov outwits 07 and carries off the death ray. End of story.

Georg* has read *Avakoum Zahov Against 07* three times. Many other Bulgarians have read it more than once. Georg has a ready reason for the book's popularity: "People read about Zahov because he was the first exciting hero to appear in a Bulgarian story in 20 years."

In Bulgaria, as in all Communist countries, the government runs the publishing companies and decides what shall be printed. Georg isn't too bothered that his government controls the arts. "Everyone needs goals to work for and guidelines to follow," says Georg. But he admits that it's boring when the only books are those that praise Communist workers. "I've read enough about comrades' winning medals at factories, growing prize crops of wheat, or breaking records for dam-building. Sometimes I like to read stories that are *not* about good Communists."

Georg is not alone among Bulgarian young people in criticizing his government, and this has the Bulgarian government worried. Few young people are preparing to take over important Party roles. And key jobs in business and industry remain unfilled, because

*These Bulgarian teen-agers serve without pay on
a road-building project in the countryside. Is this
a good idea? Or should they be able to refuse?*

these are reserved for faithful Party members.

Georg's father is disturbed at his son's criticism of
the government. "We've made great progress in the
last 20 years," he argues. "It will be sad if our best
young people don't cooperate for the good of the
country."

"The good of the country" means different things to Georg and his father. Arguments such as theirs go on in homes across Bulgaria. In this country, not much bigger than the state of Tennessee, there have been many changes since 1944. That was when the Communist Party took over the government. Bulgaria was then mostly a nation of poor farmers. The population was less than seven million. The majority could not read. There were few schools, little electricity outside the cities, and many hungry people.

Bulgarian cities were thinly settled. Most people lived on small farms in the plains. In the north, between the Danube River and the Balkans, farmers grew wheat, barley, and corn. In the central Karlovo* Valley they raised roses for perfume and plums for brandy. In the southern Maritsa* River Valley between the Balkans and the Rhodope* Mountains, they grew tobacco, fruit, and cotton.

Today the population has grown by about a million, and most Bulgarians are still farmers. But 95 percent of the farms are now under government control, as in the Soviet Union. Acting under government orders, the farmers have pooled their land, animals, and equipment into large farming operations called collectives. Run by modern methods, each collective must produce its government-set quota. Each farm worker is paid according to his collective's production rate. If the collective produces more than its quota, part of the extra "profits" are divided among the workers.

But the development of Bulgarian industry takes most of the government's attention these days. Next to Albania, Bulgaria is the least industrialized country of Eastern Europe. So the government has sent many capable men — Georg's father among them — to special schools. There they learn how to run modern fac-

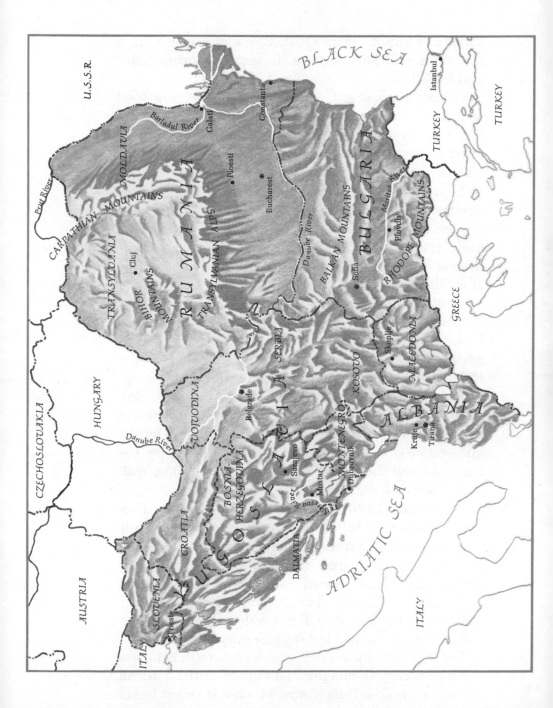

tories and mines. Georg's father now manages a large coal mine near Sofia. Coal is the most important mineral in Bulgaria.

Oil and natural gas, discovered in 1964, now feed refineries near the town of Pleven.* Bulgaria exports bicycles, motorcycles, and refrigerators. But it still must import most other manufactured products, as well as timber.

How have the collectives been able to buy new equipment? Who sets up the farm quotas? Who pays for the industrial training? Who helped design and build the new refineries? Is it the Bulgarian Communist Party, as Georg's father implies? Not really. It is "Uncle Ivan."

Uncle Ivan is the Bulgarian nickname for the Soviet Union, just as "Uncle Sam" is a nickname for the United States. Uncle Ivan has been a part of Bulgaria's history for a long time. It is believed that the Bolgars, the tribe that gave its name to Bulgaria, originated in Russia's Volga River Valley. When the Bolgars wandered west into the Balkans, they found Slavs already there. They defeated the Slavs in battle, but accepted many Slavic traditions, including the language and the Eastern Orthodox faith. Thus Bulgaria became a Slavic land.

In the late 1300's the Turks swept into the Balkans, conquering Bulgaria and settling down to rule for the next five centuries. There are still many Turks in Bulgaria. Most grow tobacco, work in metal, or weave rugs. Until recently, many Turkish children went to Turkish-run schools. Mosques, where the Moslem Turks worshiped, are scattered across Bulgaria. Many are now used only as museums.

From what remains of Turkish culture in Bulgaria today, it is easy to imagine the impact of the Turkish occupation on the Bulgarians. At what is today Lenin

✦§ Outside the cities, Bulgaria is still an old land.

Old ways continue in rural Bulgaria. This farm-wife washes her dishes under an outdoor spigot and lets her pots dry out on the rack at left.

Square in Sofia there is a strange-looking church. It was built half underground because the Turks didn't approve of the Orthodox religion. They didn't want any churches taller than Moslem mosques.

That was the way the Bulgarians had to live when the Turks ruled — half underground. Bulgarian artists had for centuries painted beautiful *ikons* (religious images). They continued to do so — but in hiding. As late as the 1700's Bulgaria had no printing presses. Monks wrote hand-lettered books on Bulgarian history and painted frescoes on church walls. Thus was Bulgarian culture kept alive.

In addition to an underground culture, there were underground fighters in Bulgaria during the long Turkish occupation. These fighters, called *haiduks,** attacked the Turks guerrilla-style whenever they had a chance. They pillaged the Turkish tax collectors. They tried to free Bulgarian boys who had been drafted into Moslem armies. The habit of guerrilla fighting established by the haiduks became a tradition of the Balkan peoples.

It was Uncle Ivan who finally stepped in to help the Bulgarians. In 1878 the Russians under Czar Alexander II joined Bulgarian fighters to defeat the Turks. Independence came in 1908. But even after regaining its independence, Bulgaria kept suffering defeat. It lost territory in the Balkan Wars of 1912. When it tried to regain the land by joining Germany in World War I, it lost once more. When World War II started, Bulgaria sided with Germany again. And when the Nazis attacked the Soviet Union, Uncle Ivan was suddenly Bulgaria's enemy.

Near the war's end, Soviet armies overran Bulgaria and installed a Communist government. Since then, Bulgaria has been closely tied to the Soviet Union. Even if they wanted to pull away, Bulgarian leaders might find it difficult. Most of Bulgaria's foreign trade is with the Soviet Union, and Bulgaria's industry depends heavily on Soviet aid.

The signs of Soviet aid are obvious in Sofia. It has many office buildings built since World War II in the "wedding cake" style that Stalin favored for Moscow. Dingy old apartment buildings are being replaced with new high-rises. But much of Sofia reflects more than the Soviet influence. Situated at the foot of the Vitosha* mountain range, Sofia is a beautiful old city. It has parks and gardens and coffee houses. It has graceful old palaces built like German castles. It has a few Moslem mosques with spindly spires called *minarets.**

Outside the cities, Bulgaria is still an old land. Here most people still travel by horse and wagon. Few roads have been built in the mountainous areas. People who live in the mountain villages hardly ever leave their communities.

Clothing is drab and expensive in Bulgaria. Georg's father pays two weeks' salary for a new suit — and he can't afford that very often. His new TV set cost two months' pay. Washing machines and other appliances can be bought only in the larger towns. When the machines break down, few know how to fix them.

There is no unemployment in Bulgaria, but pay is poor. No one goes hungry, but shoppers must wait in long lines for groceries. As in the Soviet Union, food distribution in inefficient. Nearly everyone in Bulgaria can read. But, as Georg complains, much that is published is dull, dull, dull.

Chapter 9

Rumania:
Reluctant Communists

THERE IS NO "LATE SHOW" on Rumanian TV, which is owned and directed by the government. It believes that late broadcasts would make viewers too tired for the next day's work. The government would like all workers to be in bed by midnight.

As in other Communist countries, the Communist Party not only controls the government, but also the communications media — TV, radio, newspapers, magazines, and books. It censors books, movies, plays, paintings, sculptures, and other art works.

But in Rumania, some things run differently than in other Communist countries. The censors allow jokes on the air that are highly critical of life in Rumania. At the same time, they don't permit newsmen to broadcast news reports until every sentence has been checked and printed first in the Party newspaper. Thus some news stories are three days old before going on the air.

Bucharest,* Rumania's capital, was once a rural trading town. After it became the national capital in 1859, Bucharest expanded. Rail lines linked it with Constanta, Rumania's main port on the Black Sea, and with the rest of the country. In the city a miniature Arch of Triumph was erected — a sign that Bucharest wanted to be thought of as another Paris.

During World War II, when Rumania was under Nazi German control, the city was damaged by Allied air attacks. For about 10 years after the war, the country was dominated by the Soviets, who had helped drive the Germans out in 1944. Rumania became a Communist nation, at first one of the most obedient. Today Bucharest is only starting to regain its reputation as a cultured and lively city.

The first few improvements came in the early 1960's. The government decided that Rumania should be less dependent on the U.S.S.R. It decreed that the Russian language would no longer be compulsory in Rumanian schools.

There was a further loosening of ties in the late 1960's. Tourists from Western Europe and the U.S. were encouraged to visit Rumanian resorts on the Black Sea. American companies were asked to sell their products in Rumania. More Western newsmen were permitted to report from Bucharest.

Moscow did not approve of these moves, but it did not try to prevent them. In 1968 the Rumanian government defied Moscow by not sending troops to join other East European forces invading Czechoslovakia (see page 174).

Today the Rumanian government carefully balances reforms with controls. It has increased trade with Western countries — but it continues to import raw materials from the Soviet Union. It is also building up its own industries and developing its own

High-rise accommodations for vacationing workers
crowd the beaches at this Black Sea resort in
Rumania. Tourists from the West are also welcome.

natural resources: steel, chemicals, oil, natural gas. Industrialization is changing the face of much of Rumania.

Ion* is a 16-year-old boy who lives with his parents in Ploesti* — nicknamed "Oil City." Before they came to Ploesti, they lived on a 12-acre farm in Moldavia,* Rumania's easternmost province.

130

"Sugar beets were our main crops," says Ion. "We also had fruit trees — apples, pears, and plums from which we made *tuica*,* Rumanian brandy. I helped out in the orchards after school. The Barladul* River wasn't far away. In summer my friends and I would hitch rides on barges and float all the way south to the port of Galati,* where the Barladul joins the Danube."

Rumania was mostly small farms before World War II. The farmlands were among the most fertile in Europe. The Communists who came to power after the war realized this and began to turn most farms into collectives.

Ion's parents, like many others, resisted giving up their land. But the Communist government made it hard for those who held back. After a particularly hard year, Ion's father decided to move his family to Ploesti.

Today the family lives in a forest of oil derricks. Tall metal towers rise up out of the Danubian Plain, dwarfing the brick homes and concrete apartment buildings of Ploesti. Steel pumps bob up and down all day, drawing oil out of the earth.

Together Ion's parents earn about $150 a month at the refinery. They have a new apartment — two full-sized rooms, a bathroom, and a tiny kitchen with a two-burner stove and small refrigerator. Rent is about $17 a month. They've had a TV set for a year.

And they're putting aside money to buy a Dacia.* This small car, built with the help of the French, is named after the Dacians,* the first known settlers of Rumania. The car costs about $3,000, so the family won't be able to afford it for several years.

As a city boy, Ion sees a car in his future. But another Rumanian boy of the same age can only dream. He's Alexandru,* who lives deep in the forests of

Transylvania.* His father, Vasile,* is a logger in the Bihor* Mountains. His mother, Olga,* works at a sawmill. Their combined salaries are about $100 a month.

Alexander and Vasile wear felt leggings, coarse linen shirts, sheepskin vests, wool hats, and heavy leather sandals. Around their waists are wide belts with pockets.

Olga's clothing displays her needlework skills. Her blouse is embroidered on the sleeves and cuffs, following an age-old pattern. It is tucked into a long cotton skirt, over which she wears a tight apron. On her head is a *marama,** a silk or linen scarf.

Tradition dictates dress in the Rumanian countryside. It also determines the way people build and decorate their homes. Alexandru's house is wooden, with a steep tile roof to let the snow slide off. It is decorated inside and out with intricate carvings. Tulips and lilies have been whittled into the rafters, beams, and gateposts. Circles, crosses, and stars are cut into the panels.

A few tables and chairs sit in the largest room, along with the parents' bed. A middle-sized room, divided by a screen, has a chest of drawers and two cots — one for Alexandru and one for his sister, now a nun in an Eastern Orthodox convent. In the small kitchen are a brick oven, a sink (with pitchers for carrying in water from a pump outside), and shelves for plates and cups.

Bright rugs and tapestries contrast with the plain furniture and dark walls. Woven of wool and dyed purple, red, blue, and pink, these are the pride of every Rumanian home. Olga has spent years making them. She has spread them over beds and tables and has hung many on the walls. Rugs such as these are never put on the floor.

POPULATION DISTRIBUTION
IN EASTERN EUROPE

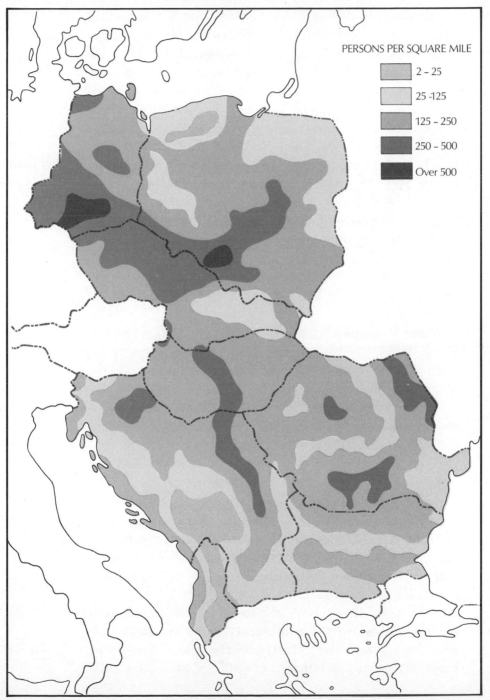

PERSONS PER SQUARE MILE

- 2 – 25
- 25 -125
- 125 – 250
- 250 – 500
- Over 500

Alexandru's family dates back to the Dacians, the people who first settled the Danubian plains ages ago. Today's Rumanian language, however, is a legacy of the Romans, conquerors of the Dacians. Very different from the Slavic languages spoken in Russia and other Eastern European lands, it is part of the Romance language family, along with Italian, French, Spanish, and Portuguese. For example, "good evening" in Rumanian is *buona seara*. In Italian it is *buona sera*; In French, *bon soir*. But in Russian it is *dobryi vetcher*.

In Transylvania, which touches Hungary, Rumanian is not the only language spoken. German-speaking people live in an area called the Banat* and in the Brasov district. Hungarians, speaking Magyar,* live in and around the city of Cluj* in the central Carpathians.*

There are also many gypsies in Transylvania. From these people — musicians, horse-traders, fortune-tellers — come colorful customs and music. Composer Georges Enesco made Transylvanian gypsy melodies famous in his "Rumanian Rhapsodies," written in the early 1900's. And the Festival of Green George originated with the gypsies.

The festival takes place on St. George's Day in late April. A young willow tree is cut down and decorated with flowers and leaves, then propped up in a prominent place. Mothers-to-be leave a piece of their clothing beneath the tree. If a leaf falls on the clothing during the night, it promises an easy childbirth. Old or sick people spit three times on the tree and pray for good health.

A young village boy is chosen to be the Green George. He is dressed completely in leaves to represent spring and the rebirth of the plant kingdom. First he throws a handful of green fodder to the cattle

From the gypsies — musicians, horse-traders, fortune-tellers — come colorful customs and music.

This Rumanian gypsy youth adds an exotic touch to the Transylvanian scene. He may be a musician, a tinker, or a trader, but he's always on the move with all his belongings in his caravan.

as a sign that they will have plenty of food in the coming year. Then he takes three nails that have been in a stream for three days and hammers them into the willow tree. He soon pulls them out and returns them to the stream. This, the villagers believe,

135

brings good fortune from the water spirits. At the festival's end, a puppet likeness of Green George is thrown into the stream.

Alexandru has taken part in several Green George festivals. But the ceremonies he knows best are those of the church he attends every Sunday with his parents.

The Rumanian Orthodox service is informal. Worshipers usually stand — there are seldom any pews in the churches. Many pray privately, paying little attention to the service. Most of the congregation are old women, dressed in black, clutching scraps of paper with names of relatives on them. These they pass forward to the priest with requests for special prayers. Their murmurs join with the low sounds of the priest's voice, the chants of the choir boys, the smell of incense, and the glistening of the gold-threaded altar cloths beneath the candles.

"Our church is seldom crowded," says Alexandru, "except on Christmas and Easter. I guess it's because so few Rumanians are interested in religion — few my age, anyway. Our Communist Party doesn't approve of religion. The Department of Cults has helped fix up some churches and monasteries, but only as tourist attractions."

The Danube River finishes its 1,725-mile course by tracing most of Rumania's southern border, collecting the waters of Carpathian and Transylvanian mountain streams along the way. Then it curves north to meet the Prut,* which flows between Rumania and the Soviet Union. Finally, muddy and slowed by silt, it soaks its way through acres of marshes and empties into the Black Sea.

At the delta, where the Danube ends, Rumanians catch sturgeon, full of roe for caviar. And there, in the great clusters of poplars, willows, and reeds, are the nests of herons, ducks, pelicans, cormorants, storks. The soil is so rich that the government has drained parts of it for farmlands.

"One day I want to go down the Danube from one end to the other," Alexandru says. "I'll go by canoe so I can get through the shallows. I'll see parts of Rumania I've always wondered about — like the Iron Gate [once a dangerous gorge in the Danube where the Rumanians and Yugoslavs have since built a dam]. And I'll pass other countries along the way — West Germany, Austria, Czechoslovakia, Hungary, Yugoslavia, Bulgaria, and a bit of the Soviet Ukraine.

"I guess I might have some trouble going by the border guards at Austria and West Germany. They might think I was trying to escape to the West. But maybe by the time I take my trip, governments won't have such strict rules."

Chapter 10

Yugoslavia: The Day the Earth Trembled

THE MORNING AFTER HIS BIRTHDAY — it was 5:15 A.M. on Friday, July 26, 1963 — Dimitrije Milanov* got out of bed to see if his new bike was still on the front porch.

At that instant, Dimitrije saw two houses across the street collapse like a house of cards. The walls wrinkled and cracked, then caved in. Bricks flew into the street. On Dimitrije's house, the side of the porch where the bike was standing suddenly slanted, and the bike rolled into a big hole that had opened up underneath. Part of the roof broke off as the walls supporting it cracked and shook.

Twenty seconds later everything was quiet. Dimitrije picked his way back into the house, through slivers of broken mirrors and overturned chairs and sprigs of blue mountain flowers once in a vase. At last he found his mother and father. They had been searching frantically for him.

This was the terrifying Skoplje* earthquake. It destroyed 90 percent of the old Turkish section of the city. Minarets toppled from mosques. Wagons were crushed under the roofs of sheds. Uprooted trees smashed houses and cars. In the central business district 75 percent of the buildings were destroyed or damaged beyond repair. The railway station roof came tumbling down, part of it on an incoming train. More than 5,000 people in Skoplje, Yugoslavia's third largest city, were killed. About 100,000 were left homeless.

Today Dimitrije is in his 20's and works as a bricklayer in the city of Mostar,* about 220 miles northwest of Skoplje. He returns to Skoplje only infrequently to see his family.

Approaching Skoplje today from the north, one sees rows of one-story houses built of rippled metal. Children play in the dusty dirt roads. One road is newly covered with a thick layer of asphalt. Small boys poke sticks into the tar bubbles along the side of the road. Their mothers, clutching string shopping bags, wait at the bus stop for a ride into the center city.

Once, soon after the quake, these houses were considered temporary. Now the people who live in them wonder if they will ever get new homes closer to the heart of Skoplje. Dimitrije and his family were lucky. Their house could be repaired after the earthquake. Dimitrije's father, who worked for a building firm at the time, helped restore the house quickly. After the quake, his company put up dozens of new apartment buildings in Skoplje.

Skoplje is a jumble of old and new, rich and poor, Moslem and Christian. There are oxcarts and automobiles, tumbledown houses and modern hotels, crumbling mosques and elaborate Orthodox churches.

139

✑ Yugoslavia contains a complex mixture of different peoples with different traditions.

Yugoslavia itself is also a jumble. It contains a complex mixture of different peoples with different traditions who, until 1918, never lived under one government. The country is made up of six separate Communist "republics": Macedonia,* Serbia,* Montenegro,* Bosnia-Herzegovina,* Croatia,* and Slovenia.* There are also two provinces, Vojvodina* and Kosmet.* The majority of the people speak Serbo-Croatian. Slovenian and Macedonian are also spoken.

Each republic controls many of its internal affairs. But the wealthier north must help support the poorer south. Moslems often chafe under rule by non-Moslems. Croats must help build roads for Serbs. And Montenegro must depend on Herzegovina for electric power. "Yugoslavia is six nations," says Dimitrije's father, "and Marshal Tito is the glue."

Tito, whose real name was Josip Broz,* became president of Yugoslavia in 1945. He had won the support of most Yugoslavs during World War II, when he led resistance fighters against the occupying Nazis. At the war's end, Tito's forces took over the country. Having spent some time in the Soviet Union before the war, he modeled his new government on the Soviet system.

But Tito's government did not follow the Soviet pattern for very long. Stalin, the Soviet dictator, began demanding the best of Yugoslavia's raw materials — copper, coal, timber, lead. He ordered Tito to

"Come join our party!" say these friendly Yugoslavs to a stranger who happens to wander by.

speed up collectivization of Yugoslav farms. When Tito refused to follow orders, Stalin called him a traitor to communism and demanded that the Yugoslavs expel their leader.

The Yugoslav Communists stuck by Tito. Thus, from 1948 on, Tito and his country were left without Soviet aid and under the threat of Soviet attack. With support from the United States and other Western nations, Yugoslavia slowly developed into one of the most prosperous and least restricted of the Communist countries of Eastern Europe.

"Because of Tito," says Dimitrije's father, "ours was the first Communist country to do away with the secret police. We were the first to abolish collectivization of farms too, and the first to plan factory production to suit the needs of the consumer."

Dimitrije has a somewhat different opinion of Tito. "Hotels go up before houses and apartment buildings. Tourists get fancy suites for their vacation stays. But the people of Mostar — we don't have room enough to breathe in our crowded homes."

The government's "open door" policy allows Yugoslavs to travel abroad. Through the same "open door" comes a yearly flood of foreign visitors to Yugoslavia. Many Yugoslavs profit from this booming tourist industry.

Dimitrije is one of them. He earns extra money by jumping from Mostar's 60-foot Old Bridge into the narrow Neretva* River. Tourist parties pay him about a dollar to see him risk his neck.

He makes the leap as dramatic as possible. First he paces the bridge, casting dark glances at the rocks in the river below. Then he draws back, pretending

On their way between Sarajevo and the Adriatic Sea, travelers cross Mostar's historic Old Bridge.

he's afraid to jump. At last he stands on the rail, mumbles a prayer, and leaps.

The tourists press close to the railing. "Where is he?" they ask. "Maybe he's struck a rock!"

Then a hand emerges, followed by a head. Dimitrije has surfaced 150 yards downstream. He smiles at the onlookers and swims to shore. Once on the bank, he shakes the water of the Neretva from his hair and hurries back to the Old Bridge to await the next batch of tourists.

Mostar, meaning "old bridge," is the chief city of Herzegovina. It is located halfway between the Adriatic Sea and the Bosnian city of Sarajevo.* Before the Old Bridge was built by the Turks, Mostar was just a small village along one side of the Neretva. Then, in 1566, the stone span was completed, changing the fortunes of the village.

Mostar soon became the main link between Sarajevo and the coast. Enterprising men came to develop the area's forests and minerals. Leather dressers and tailors followed, forming prosperous guilds. Traders from Asia Minor brought gold to Mostar. Craftsmen set up shops along the river to work the gold into cups, plates, and bracelets.

The Turks made Mostar a military base for the defense of the Neretva Valley. The Austrians, who ruled the region after the Turks were driven out, built a railroad that tied Mostar close to the other trading centers. As the 1900's began, Mostar became a secret headquarters of Serbian nationalists plotting to free all Serbs from Austrian control.

Then, in 1914, a young Serbian shot the son of Austria's emperor in Sarajevo. Soon, the world was plunged into its first World War (see page 153). Mostar's fortunes, like everyone else's, took a bloody turn. After the war, there was a brief spurt of prosperity, but then came the worldwide Depression of the 1930's and World War II.

The Turks left Mostar nearly a century ago, but a majority of the Slavic townspeople are still Moslems. At dusk there is a curious mixture of sounds in the air — hotel orchestra playing pop tunes and *muezzins** (Moslem religious men) standing atop the minarets, calling the faithful to worship.

Yugoslavia's most prosperous farmers are in the rich lowlands of the north, the Vojvodina region of Serbia. There farmers can rent modern machinery from government cooperatives and get advice from experts on the best use of the land. Or they can actually join the cooperatives themselves. Their region alone produces enough corn and wheat to supply all of Yugoslavia.

But in the Neretva Valley farming is a different story. The soil is poor. The limestone rock seems to swallow the rain before it gets to the crops. The government has had a hard time trying to set up cooperatives. So the Mostar farmers continue to work their own small, scattered plots.

Mostar is a market for peasant farmers of the Neretva Valley. Early Monday mornings, the farmers load their carts with the week's harvest — plums, cherries, melons, sugar beets, potatoes, hay — and head for town. In the Mostar marketplace they spread their produce on long tables, then settle in for a day of bargaining with shoppers.

"Some things are improving," says Dimitrije. "The farmers' houses, even the ones with dirt floors, have electricity now. Some houses have running water. Most families have radios. And all their kids come to school in Mostar. But when they are graduated, they rarely go back to the farms. They go where things are happening — out to the coast, up north."

Chapter 11

Albania: Land of the Eagle

"PLEASE DON'T GIVE CANDY or clothing to the children of Albania. If you do, the Albanians will call it a Yugoslav trick."

That's a guide speaking aboard a bus entering Albania from Yugoslavia. His warning reminds the riders that Albanians and Yugoslavs have been quarreling for years about the border they share and about the people who live in the border area.

The road that crosses the border is narrow and bumpy. When the bus nears the edge of the mountain road, the riders can see a gray-blue stream far below. Beyond the stream stretch low rocky hills covered with scrub pine. As the bus bumps onward, high mountains rise in the distance. These are the Albanian Alps.

Albania is a small country, made up mostly of mountains. The mountains have kept the people isolated and kept alive their ancient customs — and sometimes feuds. Albania is called the "Land of the

Eagle" — perhaps because the eagle is the creature best fitted for life here.

The Communist government allows foreign visitors into the country only in small groups, and then strictly limits their travels. Native Albanians have trouble getting around too. Only diplomats and certain other government officials are permitted to leave the country. And Albania has only 100 miles of railroad (all built since World War II). This railroad connects the Adriatic Sea with the capital city of Tirana* and a few towns in between. There are no rail links with Albania's neighbors — Yugoslavia to the north and east, or Greece to the south.

New asphalt roads are being built through the mountains, but most old ones remain unpaved and full of potholes. There is an airport in Tirana, but there are few direct flights from Western cities.

Ordinary Albanians don't seem too concerned about their isolation. "Who needs roads?" an old man asks in Kruje,* a mountain town. "I can count on my fingers the people in town who have a car." Laughing heartily, he settles back in his chair at a café to drink a cup of thick Turkish coffee.

Life in this old town appears little affected by the 20th century. Women in long dark skirts and white hooded shawls carry sacks of cheese and vegetables slung over their shoulders. Some stop at the government bulletin board near the café — the daily news report for most. Other women move on to the square to spread blankets on the ground and arrange their foodstuffs for sale. All day long small children run through the dusty pebbled streets.

In the very center of Kruje, there is a bronze statue of a man on a horse. It reads "Skanderbeg" in large letters, and beneath tells the story of this hero of Kruje.

In the 15th century, a nine-year-old son of a Kruje nobleman was kidnapped by the Turks. The Turks, already conquerors of most of the Balkan lands, wanted to add Albania to their empire. Since Kruje was a fortress town and home of powerful princes, it was a prime target. The boy was taken to the Turkish sultan's court.

The Turks gave him the name Skanderbeg. When he grew to manhood, they trained him to command Turkish troops. One day Skanderbeg heard that the Albanians were rising against the Turkish invaders. He deserted the sultan's forces and went home to lead the people of his native land.

For the next 25 years Skanderbeg's small bands of fierce Albanian fighters kept large Turkish armies from overrunning the land. Only after he died, in 1468, did Albania fall completely to the Turks — to be ruled by them for more than 400 years.

If Skanderbeg were suddenly to climb down from his bronze horse today and mix with the people of Kruje, he'd probably go unnoticed. For many of the *Ghegs** (northern Albanians) and *Tosks** (southern Albanians) in mountain villages dress as their ancestors did 500 years ago.

Many of the men are bearded. They wear a small white felt hat, shaped either like a pillbox or half an eggshell, depending on the region. On most days they wear wide trousers and coarsely woven shirts, with sashes about their waists. On special days the Gheg men wear red-and-yellow vests and narrow trousers edged in black. The Tosks don knee-length pants with long woolen stockings, embroidered shirts, and decorated belts.

Women of both groups wear scarves — white ones if they are married. They also wear much jewelry — usually long strings of beads or pieces of jingling

*In this photo of a Tirana marketplace, what do
you see that reminds you of the West? What is
typically East European? What is absent that
you might think would be in such a marketplace?*

metal. Moslem women wear long-sleeved blouses
tucked into wide trousers drawn in at the ankles.
Christian women wear similar blouses and full skirts.

Only in the larger towns and cities of Albania are
foreign influences seen. Business suits, dresses, and
skirts in Western styles are worn on the streets.
Stores sell toothpaste, cosmetics, and shopping bags
made in China. Plays by Soviet writers are performed

149

by the Albanian National Theater. Magazines and books from China and Eastern Europe sometimes appear next to Albanian publications in libraries and bookstores. Sometimes the contrast between the foreign magazines and the Albanian reality can be quite disturbing.

"If I wore a skirt as short as the ones I see in Polish magazines, I'm sure I'd be fired," says Gjeta,* a 17-year-old girl who lives in Tirana. "Besides, my parents are strict Moslems. They believe that women should be covered up when they appear in public. Until recently, my mother always wore a veil over her face when she went out. She'd never approve of a short skirt. And neither do I. None of my friends wear skirts above their knees either."

Gjeta sees Polish and Czech magazines at the museum in Tirana where she works as assistant to the director. The museum exhibits folk art from all over Albania. It also displays a large collection of archaeological findings dug up in modern times by Albanian farmers. These objects were probably made by the Illyrians,* a people who settled on the Adriatic coast in about the fourth century B.C.

The Albanians are directly descended from the Illyrians. They were conquered by the Romans, then by the Normans, and by other foreign powers through the centuries. In the 1400's, the Turks took over.

That was when most Albanians became Moslems. The Turks converted most of the Catholic and Orthodox churches to mosques. They taught the women to cook Turkish recipes — eggplant with chilies, and cerkas* (boiled chicken with nut sauce). They also forbade Christian scholars to write books. So Albanian poets composed long ballads about great Albanian deeds that were handed down by word of mouth from parents to children.

150

The Turks were not finally driven out until 1912, when Albania declared its independence. But because it was weak and sought by its neighbors, the big European powers appointed a foreign prince, a German, as ruler. He deserted Albania when World War I began, and in his place came foreign armies.

After the war an Albanian made himself president, then king. He was Zog* I. King Zog was a dictator who tried to build up Albania's economy by inviting Italian companies in. But when World War II broke out, the Italians seized the government. At this time Enver Hoxha* formed the Albanian Communist Party. When World War II ended and the Italians were defeated, Hoxha and his Communists came to power.

Albania remains the poorest of the Balkan nations and of all Europe. Most of its people can't fight their way above the poverty level. Party Chief Hoxha, in an angry political dispute in the 1960's, broke with the Soviet Union, until then a major source of aid to Albania. Since that time, Hoxha's country has had to depend on China, thousands of miles away, for money, machines, and food.

Albania is also by far the strictest of the Communist governments of Eastern Europe. Its government, backed by a Stalinist secret police, forbids free expression of any kind. Its favorite slogans are "Callouses on the Hands of the Workers" and "Glory to Marx and Lenin."

These days, when masses of noisy young people march through Tirana's wide, empty streets, they are not assembling to protest. They have most likely been ordered out to cheer a new shipment of potato seeds from China. "What the people need," says an Albanian official, "the Party furnishes — what the Party says, the people do."

Police seize the assassins of Archduke Francis Ferdinand of Austria and his wife. Murders soon led to World War I.

THE SPARK THAT ENGULFED EUROPE

WARS DON'T JUST HAPPEN. They are always the result of a long history of quarrels and grievances, just and unjust. World War I came after long decades of general peace in Europe. But those same decades were pockmarked by an almost constant series of local wars, revolutions, territorial take-overs, and uprisings all over the continent.

152

Nowhere was this European turbulence more pronounced than in the Balkans. There the warring and feuding became so intense that the name "Balkans" came to be associated with upheaval and violence. Similarly, the term "Balkanization" was coined. Its meaning: the breakup of a large area into small, weak, and frequently feuding states.

One of the causes of Balkanization was the decline of the Ottoman* Empire. At its height, the Ottoman Empire had sprawled across most of Southeast Europe, biting deep into Poland and Russia. But by the 1800's the Ottoman Empire was the "sick man of Europe." In particular, its hold on the Balkans and surrounding lands steadily diminished throughout the 19th century.

In 1912 and 1913, two wars, known to history as the Balkan Wars, were fought over the spoils of the dying Ottoman Empire. The actual issues which sparked the wars, and the secret diplomacy and in-fighting which accompanied the wars, are extremely complex — and not all that important. What is important is that alliances constantly broke up and formed again, and ancient feuds were renewed. Soon the larger powers of Europe began to conclude that the small Balkan nations would have to be punished for the trouble they were making.

For the major powers were beginning to worry that the tinderbox of the Balkans could ignite all of Europe. And Europe was ready to be set aflame. It needed only a spark from some such place as the Balkans to start the fire. In June 1914, only 10 months after the Second Balkan War was settled, that spark was generated — again in the Balkans.

It happened this way: Bosnia (which is today one of the republics within Yugoslavia) was then part of Austria. Its capital city was Sarajevo, which was preparing for a visit from the Austrian Archduke Francis Ferdinand and his wife. The Archduke was heir to the throne. But a plot was brewing to assassinate him.

The plotters were members of the Serbian Black Hand, an organization dedicated to increasing Serbia's strength

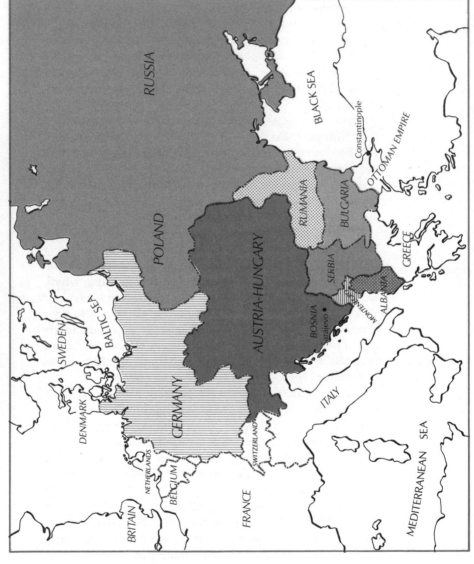

EASTERN EUROPE in 1914

BRITAIN

NETHERLANDS

BELGIUM

FRANCE

SWITZERLAND

DENMARK

GERMANY

SWEDEN

BALTIC SEA

POLAND

RUSSIA

AUSTRIA-HUNGARY

ITALY

BOSNIA
Sarajevo

MONTENEGRO

SERBIA

ALBANIA

RUMANIA

BULGARIA

GREECE

BLACK SEA

Constantinople

OTTOMAN EMPIRE

MEDITERRANEAN SEA

and position. They were ready to kill Francis Ferdinand because he wanted to swallow up much of Serbia in his own Austro-Hungarian empire. At least six youths were assigned the assassination task.

On June 28 the royal couple were riding along the old streets of Sarajevo — but without the police or military protection they should have had. One of the would-be killers hurled a bomb at them. It missed, wounding several spectators. Nevertheless, the royal automobile proceeded toward the municipal building, where the mayor was waiting to welcome them in a public ceremony.

After the ceremony was over, the Archduke and his wife started to renew their tour. Another of the youths fired two shots, killing the royal pair — and starting a train of events which led to World War I.

The war started because Austria was now determined to stop Serbia's dream of expansion. It made strict demands on Serbia, and when Serbia would not meet them, Austria declared war. Russia leaped into the war on Serbia's side to support its fellow Slavs and to punish Austria. More reluctantly, Germany joined its ally, Austria, in the fighting.

Germany also declared war on France, which had long been allied by treaty with Russia. In attacking France, the German armies also invaded Belgium, which was officially neutral, although it was friendly with Britain. Seeing this, Britain declared war on Germany.

By August 1914 virtually all of Europe was ablaze. The spark struck in the Balkans had spread into a titanic fire and the flames would not be stilled until millions of lives had been lost.

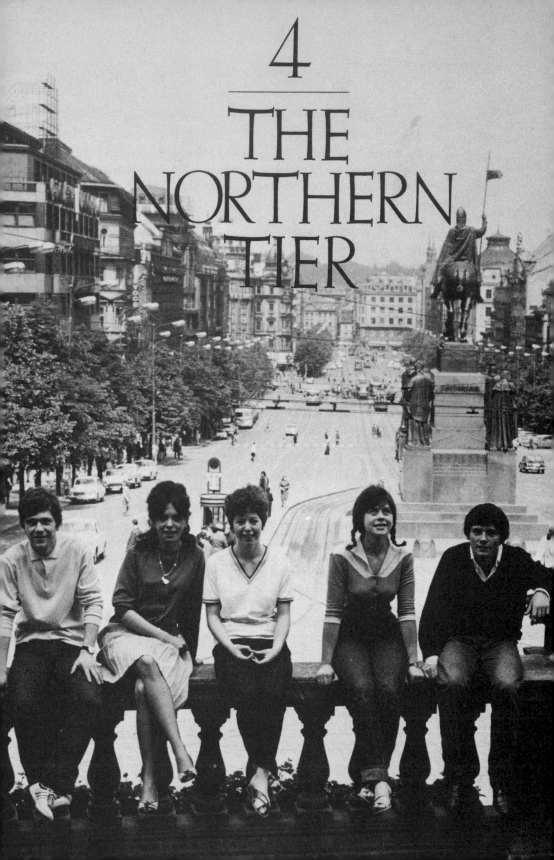

4
THE NORTHERN TIER

Chapter 12

Poland:
The Black Madonna Lives

THE NATIONS OF THE BALKANS and the Soviet Union all are heavily influenced by the East. Three fourths of the Soviet Union lies in Asia. Moreover, the Asian influence is strong, even in the European part of the country. In Moscow, for example, the onion-shaped churches give an Oriental look to the whole city.

The Balkan countries were occupied by the Turks for centuries, and they too show the influence of Eastern history. Moslem culture made a deep imprint on Yugoslavia, Albania, Rumania, and Bulgaria.

But the four countries that make up the "Northern Tier" of Communist Eastern Europe — Hungary, Czechoslovakia, Poland, and East Germany — are much closer to Western Europe than to the East in their history and outlook.

To be sure, they all look to the Soviet Union for leadership. They also all have dedicated Communist

157

◆§ Despite the Party's efforts to discourage worship, the Poles have the strongest church ties of any Communist nation in the world.

Roman Catholicism is strong and thriving in Communist Poland. Here a bishop blesses the faithful.

governments. Still, these Northern Tier countries are geographically close to the West. And their cultures and societies are in many ways closer to their Western neighbors than to their Eastern ones.

Unlike the Soviet Union and most of the Balkan nations, the countries of the Northern Tier have close

158

trade ties with the West. And tighter than the trade ties are the blood ties. Before the end of World War II, when these nations were not yet Communist-ruled, they sent many immigrants to the West, especially to the United States. Today the ties between the people of the Northern Tier countries and their relatives in the West remain strong. There is a wide gap in political philosophy between the two sides, but there are also many strong bridges spanning that gap.

☆ ☆ ☆ ☆ ☆ ☆ ☆ ☆ ☆

St. Luke himself is said to have painted Poland's Black Madonna. The portrait of the Blessed Virgin is framed in gold and almost covered with silver, and is set above an altar where great waxen candles burn day and night. To this altar, in a monastery church in Czestochowa,* come nearly a hundred thousand Poles each August to pray before the Madonna and receive the cardinal's blessing.

Czestochowa is a symbol of the remarkable strength of religion in a country run by the Communists since 1947. Despite the Party's efforts to discourage worship, the Poles — 90 percent of them Roman Catholic — have the strongest church ties of any Communist nation in the world.

Czestochowa is also a symbol of national pride. Here, in 1655, the Poles defeated a great Swedish army threatening to overrun the entire country. Twenty-eight years later, in 1683, another high point was reached when King Jan Sobieski* defeated a Turkish army at Vienna, saving central Europe from conquest by the Turks.

But in later years the Poles were on the losing side. In 1772 Poland was split up and parts were parceled out to Russia, Prussia, and Austria. In 1793 Prussia

159

and Russia took other pieces of Poland. Finally in 1795, the three partners divided up what was left, and the name Poland disappeared from the map. It did not reappear as an independent state until the end of World War I.

"I think that the partitioning of our country made our people more patriotic," says Maria, a college student in Warsaw. "Some Poles were exiled to Siberia. Some went to France or America. Those who stayed were often forbidden to speak Polish. But our spirit never broke, and great men fought for us — men such as Kosciuszko."

Tadeusz Kosciuszko* (1746-1817) is both an American and a Polish hero. He came to America as a young man and fought in the Revolution under General Washington. He helped build a chain across the Hudson to keep the English from sailing up the river. He planned and constructed American forts, and he persuaded Thomas Jefferson to build the U.S. Military Academy at West Point.

When he learned that Poland was being divided up among foreign countries, Kosciuszko returned to his native city, Krakow.* There he raised an army of peasants and old soldiers. They defeated the invading Russians three times. Then they were crushed by superior forces and the pieces of Poland were parceled out. Released after two years, Kosciuszko spent his life trying to organize world support for Poland.

Many Poles visit the mound of earth that honors Kosciuszko in Krakow. They come to see other things too, for Krakow is called the "City of Kings." In many ways, it symbolizes Polish history.

Krakow is on the Vistula River in the southeastern corner of Poland. It was founded in the 700's by an early Slavic tribe. These Slavs lived in an area known as the "pole," or "open country," and their land

LAND USE IN EASTERN EUROPE

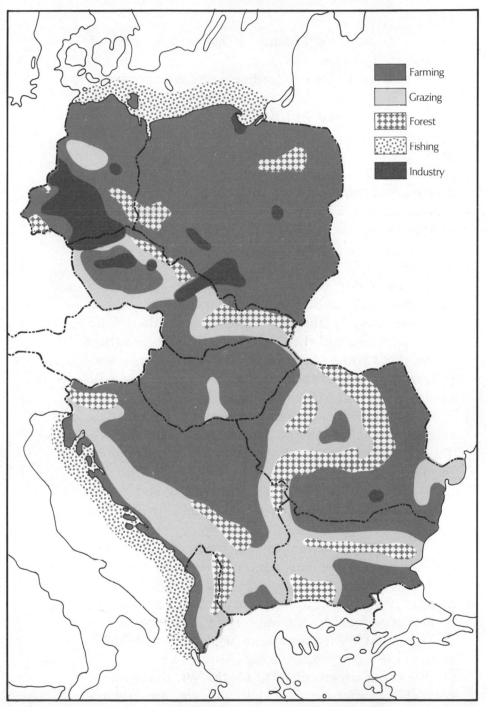

Farming
Grazing
Forest
Fishing
Industry

became known as Poland. Krakow was one of Poland's first towns.

Krakow grew into a leading cultural and trade center. For 300 years, it was Poland's capital. Casimir the Great (1309-70) founded one of Europe's first universities in Krakow in 1364. The great Polish astronomer, Copernicus* (Nikolaj Kopernik,* 1473-1543) pioneered studies which indicated that the earth and the other planets revolve around the sun. The discovery marked the beginning of Poland's golden age. In the years following, the University of Krakow became the hub of learning for all of central Europe.

Krakow today is not too different in appearance from the Krakow of the golden age. Many of the buildings have withstood wars and weather. The Castle of Kings and the Cathedral still stand as they did in the 1300's. The old houses of the clergy and judges, the old churches, and the Cloth Hall are still landmarks of the Market Square.

Polish embroidery is famous. Flowers and geometric designs are traced by silk threads of many colors. They decorate clothes worn by modern Poles only for festivals and holidays. But these same people hang embroidered cloths on their walls and cover their floors with woven rugs of bright traditional designs.

This weaving and embroidery lends a bright touch to what many Poles consider an exceedingly dull and drab life. Many Poles believe that things in their country are just not as they should be. But they become discouraged by the opposition they meet.

Maria, the Warsaw college student, wrote these words in her diary months ago:

"We often dream of lofty ideals. We think about how they could be realized, but we are always

162

Merchants have been selling their wares in Krakow's Cloth Hall for six centuries. In booths behind the stone arches, shoppers find wooden plates, walking sticks, fringed scarves, skirts, tapestries, aprons, ribbons, embroidered vests.

163

frustrated by the political situation. We begin to ask ourselves: What's the point of it all? We won't live very long anyhow, so the thing is to have a good time and forget important matters."

Maria was feeling very low when she wrote this. Her friend, Adam, was on trial for having taken part in demonstrations at the university against Soviet influence. At first she thought he was heading for prison. In the end, however, he was given a year's suspension from the university.

"You should be thankful that it is no worse for Adam. Perhaps he can get a job until he returns to school," says Maria's mother, whose name is Alina.*

Alina lived through World War II in Warsaw with her husband, who is now dead. Maria knows little about the war except for the many monuments to the dead in Warsaw today.

But Alina remembers it all. She recalls, for example, what happened to the Polish Jews. After the Nazis had taken Warsaw in 1939, they brought 500,000 Polish Jews to Warsaw. The Jews were crowded into the already bomb-damaged ghetto, which was then walled in. Their scanty diet was black bread and potatoes.

Those who did not die of starvation or disease in the ghetto were trucked out of Warsaw to special "camps" where they were put in gas chambers or shot to death. In April 1943 those few who remained alive in the ghetto put up a heroic but hopeless struggle. They carried out a series of courageous attacks on their Nazi oppressors. They were not put down until the Nazis totally destroyed the ghetto, house by house.

A year later the Polish army staged its own uprising. It too was crushed by the Germans, and Warsaw lay in ruins. When the Soviet army entered

Warsaw after Germany's surrender, it found 25,000 graves in the streets, plus tens of thousands of unexploded mines and missiles in the rubble. There was no electricity, gas, or water. Of the six million Polish civilians killed by the Nazis, about 700,000 died in Warsaw alone.

☆　☆　☆　☆　☆　☆　☆　☆　☆

Today Warsaw is a modern city, rebuilt almost from scratch. Some of its buildings — the huge Palace of Culture and Science, for example — are the elaborate "wedding cake" style set by the Soviet dictator, Stalin.

But one section of Warsaw is a reminder of the old Poland. This is the Old Town. A small district in the heart of the modern city, it centers around a cobblestone square. Old Town was destroyed with the rest of Warsaw during the war and had to be reconstructed in part from the way it looked in old paintings.

Alina runs a restaurant in Old Town, and she and Maria live above it. One of the front windows is made of bits of stained glass found in the rubble of the old Old Town. A steady stream of people every night come to eat *barszcz** (beet soup) or *grzybowa** (a soup of chopped mushrooms with cream), and *karp pu polsku** (carp with veal and egg stuffing) or *nalesziki** (pastries filled with chopped beef, rice, potato, egg, mushrooms, and onions).

Alina, who owns the restaurant, is concerned and annoyed because the government makes restaurant owners keep incredibly detailed records. They have so many forms to fill out each day, she says, that they hardly have time to plan menus or order food.

"I don't know how they expect us to make a profit," Alina snaps, "if they don't let us run our places

165

in our own way. If this restaurant isn't successful, I'll leave Warsaw and go back to my family home in the High Tatra Mountains."

If Alina moved to the High Tatras, she'd be running against the tide. More and more Poles have been moving to the cities since the end of World War II. Before the war, two thirds of the people were farmers.

After the war's destruction, many Poles left the villages and small towns to start new lives in the cities. Part of this flow came because the government tried to turn the privately owned farms into collectives. New laws required farmers to deliver much of their harvest to the government.

Many farmers did all they could to resist collectivization. At the same time, the collective farm workers complained of low living standards and too-strict police rule. In 1956 resentment grew into riots. The Communist Party was forced to change its policies.

Collectivization was stopped, and Poland today has the greatest number of privately owned farms of any Communist nation. More religious freedom was permitted. Foreign books and movies were allowed in small numbers.

If Alina goes to the High Tatras, she will probably become involved in one of Poland's most promising new industries — tourism. The High Tatras, according to Alina, are "next to heaven" because they have so much sunshine, pure air, and wild mountain scenery.

Alina and Maria have taken a raft trip twice down the Dunajec* River. They rode in one of four hollowed-out tree-trunk canoes lashed together and steered by guides. "On a voyage like that," says Alina, "it's possible to believe that politics are no more important than a rock in the river."

Chapter 13

Czechoslovakia: Waiting for the Bus That Never Comes

To reach the house where Miroslav* was born, you must walk up a hill for half a mile along a rock-strewn dirt road. It's a difficult walk, but in good weather the walk is pleasant. Firs and spruces and juniper trees all around keep the air cool and refreshing.

At the top of the hill, you come upon the house, framed by the High Tatra Mountains. Beyond the mountains is Poland. The mountains — jagged, gray, and patched with snow — span the whole horizon.

Miroslav's old house is tiny. Its bottom story is made of stone. Its upper story, made of wood, juts out about a foot. There are five other houses nearby, each with its own fields of barley, oats, and potatoes — the only crops that grow well in the thin soil of the mountains.

When Miroslav's grandparents built the house in the late 1800's, their land was their own. Today the land is owned by the Czechoslovak government. The farmers, like so many in other Communist nations, work their fields collectively. They share equipment and labor, and must give part of their produce to the Slovak Ministry of Agriculture.

Slovakia, land of the Slovaks, is the poorest of the three regions that make up Czechoslovakia. Bohemia* and Moravia,* the other two regions, have big industries and more prosperous people. But Slovakia is a land of peasants, with many more farms than factories. It was ruled by Hungary for almost 900 years. Its architecture, its music, and its cooking show the Hungarian influence. The Bohemians and Moravians speak the Czech language, but the Slovaks speak their own (but similar) Slovakian language.

It was to escape poverty that Miroslav left the house in the Tatras when he was 18. He went south to Bratislava,* on the Danube River, capital of the region. The city was already prospering as a port for Austrian and Hungarian tankers.

But Miroslav had been a farm boy with only six years of school. There were few job opportunities in Bratislava. He knew he must go elsewhere to find steady work — especially as he had met a pretty Bratislava girl named Marie and wanted to marry her. So he and Marie decided to get married and then head for a mining or manufacturing town in Moravia or Bohemia.

Marie's family, who lived in a small town near Bratislava, gave the couple a traditional country wedding. The night before the wedding, Marie's friends gathered at her house and prepared a wedding crown of apple blossoms and rosemary. They gave her whole grains of corn to hold in her mouth before

At a shepherd's hut in the High Tatras, an old woman bustles indoors with a pot of water.

the ceremony. These were to make sure she'd be a good housewife.

On the wedding day Miroslav dressed in kidskin breeches, boots, a wide-sleeved blouse, and an embroidered vest. With Marie's cousins he approached the bride's house, and, according to custom, found the door locked. Only after he had made a long formal speech to Marie's father was the door opened.

Marie was dressed in a pleated skirt of white lace, an embroidered blouse, a blue vest, and black felt boots. When the crown was placed in her hair, she asked her parents' blessing, then joined Miroslav outside. The party went to the church, where a Roman Catholic priest celebrated the marriage.

Returning to the house, Marie and Miroslav were greeted by her parents with gifts of bread and salt. These signified that the couple should never be poor. Then everyone joined in the feast, eating lamb and mutton, drinking wine, and dancing circle dances.

Marie and Miroslav settled in Plzen,* a city in Bohemia. Miroslav got a job at the V.I. Lenin (formerly Skoda) Works, where autos, locomotives, and heavy machinery are made. Marie went to work in a brewery. Miroslav's company provided an apartment near the plant for its workers. It also promised training for a better job if Miroslav proved a good worker.

Today Miroslav is a foreman of one of the largest assembly divisions of the automobile plant. Marie is a supervisor in the bottling department of the brewery. Their combined salaries add up to about $3,500 a year.

They live on the bottom floor of a three-story house outside Plzen, where they moved when Hedy, their daughter, was born. Their apartment has four rooms, brightened by Slovakian plates and carved

wooden figures from Marie's family home. Lace spreads made by Marie's grandmother cover the beds. Marie has painted a row of flowers above the stone fireplace. A cage with two canaries stands near a window.

"I can't complain about the way we live," says Marie. "We have much more than my parents ever had — running water, a refrigerator, free medical care, a pension when we're old, even a TV. It would be wonderful to have a car. But even the one made right here in Plzen costs more than two years' pay. We get around well enough on buses."

The important thing to Marie and Miroslav is Hedy's education. "We've tried to give her the things we missed when we were young. This means that we must do without some things now. But we still enjoy ourselves, especially at the movies or the theater.

"We get to Prague* a few times each year too. It's only 60 miles from here, and such a beautiful city. But I wouldn't want to live there. It's too noisy, too expensive, and too big for me. The last time we were there, for example, hundreds of young people were out in Wenceslas* Square, dressed in strange costumes. It was crazy. I still don't know what to make of it."

Jiri,* a Praguer for all his 19 years, could have told Marie what was going on. He was in Wenceslas Square that day in a bathrobe with a sign that read "Stomach Trouble." His friend was wearing pajamas and a sign saying "Sleeping Sickness."

Altogether there were about 500 young people in the Square, claiming to be ill or disabled. They were taking part in the "School's Out Spree" — an annual celebration in which most of Prague's high school seniors pretend they are too sick to go to school. They make signs describing their condition,

172

❧ There was no fighting. The invaders overpowered the Czechs by their presence alone.

Prague 1968: Why are tanks on the streets of this beautiful city? What exchange do you think is going on between soldier and civilian?

dress in bandages and nightclothes, and meet on Wenceslas Square to play hooky.

Wenceslas Square is the hub of modern Prague. From there residential sections spread out in all directions — on both sides of the Vltava* River and up the hills that surround the capital. But the Old Town was once the real heart of the city. Businesses still thrive there, and the streets are lined with historical monuments to Prague's past.

Jiri lives across the Charles Bridge from the Old Town, in an apartment with his parents and sister. He is now a student at Prague's Charles University. The School's Out Spree seems a long time ago.

Even longer ago, but far more vivid in Jiri's parents' minds, was the ending of "Prague's Spring." This unhappy event took place in August 1968.

Prague's Spring was the name given to a series of reforms brought by a Czechoslovak leader named Alexander Dubcek.* For months this man tried to shape a new kind of communism for his country. He called it "socialism with a human face." He restored freedoms — of speech, press, religion — that had been severely restricted. He relaxed travel curbs. He weakened the power of the secret police. His policies indicated continuing reforms.

But the reforms seemed too drastic to the Soviet bosses. They called up troops and tanks from Poland, East Germany, Hungary, Bulgaria, and added their own forces — about 650,000 men in all. Then they rolled across the Czechoslovakian border and into Prague. There was no fighting. The invaders overpowered the Czechs by their presence alone. Prague's Spring turned back to winter.

In the next few months the Communist grip tightened on Czechoslovakia. Under Soviet pressure, the Czech Communist Party fired Dubcek, who went into retirement. Freedoms of speech and press were tightly restricted.

Being under a foreign thumb was nothing new to Czechoslovakia. Until 1918 it had been under Austrian or Hungarian rule for centuries. Then a pair of Czech college professors, Dr. Thomas Masaryk*

174

and Dr. Edward Benes,* rallied support among the victorious World War I Allies for an independent Czechoslovakia. The new country came into being just as the war ended. Masaryk became the first president and Benes the foreign minister.

From the first, Czechoslovakia was plagued by the demands of its various nationalities. The Slovaks wanted to govern themselves. The Hungarians wanted to rejoin Hungary. Most demanding of all were the three million Germans who lived in an area of Czechoslovakia known as the Sudetenland. Most wanted to join Germany.

When the Nazis came to power in Germany in 1933, they soon began quarreling with Czechoslovakia over the issue of the Sudeten Germans. In 1938 Adolf Hitler took over the Sudetenland. Then in March 1939 he seized Bohemia and Moravia, and set up Slovakia as an "independent" state under German "protection." World War II began the following September.

By 1944 the tide had turned. Soviet armies drove westward, ridding Eastern Europe of Nazi control. But Eastern Europe was not to be free. The Soviet bosses took the place of the Nazi masters.

Many in Czechoslovakia tried hard to bring back the democracy the country had known before World War II. But the Czech Communists took control and set up a Soviet-style government. One of the last of the old democratic officials was the foreign minister, Jan Masaryk, son of Czechoslovakia's first president. In 1948 his dead body was found in the courtyard of the foreign ministry. It is believed that he either was pushed out of a window by the secret police or leaped to his death in protest against the Communist take-over of Czechoslovakia.

Life was grim in the years after World War II.

Food was scarce. Yet the Soviet authorities demanded that the Czechs concentrate on developing new heavy industries.

Jiri's father, in those days, was discouraged about his job. As a program director at a radio station, he was fairly well paid. But the government permitted only news broadcasts that were prepared by Communist Party officials. Other programs were limited to folk music, classical music by Czech composers, and Russian-language lessons. Jiri's father could not express his own ideas. He had no personal control over his work.

Then in the 1960's the government began to lift some of its restrictions on writers and artists. Filmmakers, writers, and commentators took advantage of the new freedom to criticize the government and even the Soviet Union.

This period of relative freedom peaked in 1968, when Alexander Dubcek served as Communist Party secretary. But it was at this point that Moscow, afraid that other Communist capitals might copy Prague's reforms, sent troops and tanks from many Communist countries into Czechoslovakia and overthrew Dubcek's government.

"We had sweet, sweet dreams of freedom," says Jiri's father sadly. "But after the invasion, we lost hope. It's like standing at a deserted bus stop, waiting for a bus that never comes."

Chapter 14

Hungary:
Flower on the Brim

EVA'S HUSBAND was first violinist with the Budapest* Symphony Orchestra for many years. After
he died, Eva — a fine violinist herself — taught music
at the Franz Liszt Academy. Then she was offered a
job as manager of a bookstore in Budapest, Hungary's capital. A practical woman as well as a lover of
books, she took the job. After all, she had two father-
less children to support.

The bookstore, on a busy street just off Budapest's
Great Boulevard, is always crowded. It attracts tourists, shoppers, and even businessmen. It also draws
young people from a nearby coffeehouse.

The shop is on the ground floor of a narrow stone
building put up in 1896. Two tall windows on the
second floor open onto a small balcony that juts out
over the sidewalk. On either side of the balcony are
two gargoyles (monster heads of stone). The gargoyles are one of the store's trademarks.

Another trademark is Eva herself. Customers address her respectfully by her first name. She has a long face with broad cheekbones and wrinkles around her eyes. Her silver-rimmed spectacles usually ride halfway down her nose. New customers are usually a little shy of her. But she smiles warmly and says, "*Szervusz** [how do you do]. I am happy to help you. My name is Eva."

"Sometimes I think Mama would like to give away all our books," says her daughter Magda.* "She loves her customers as much as they love her. But we need every *forint** [about five cents] we can get."

Magda is 21. She attended the University of Budapest for a year, then left to help run the bookstore. Her brother, Sandor,* 13, is still in school. The three live in a two-room apartment about a mile from the bookstore.

The store is open six days a week, from 10 to six. Each day Magda leaves the store at five to go marketing. Almost everyone in Budapest goes food shopping daily, partly because few homes have refrigeration. Magda enjoys the afternoon errands because she has a chance to see the city.

Budapest is really two connected cities. Buda, on the west bank of the Danube River, is built on and around several big hills. It is the older of the two. Pest is on the east bank. The two are linked by eight bridges.

Though Magda went to the University of Budapest in Buda, she doesn't get back to that part of the city very often. She and Sandor used to take weekend trips to Buda's Varhegy* (Castle Hill). There they visited the old royal castle. And they poked

Young Pioneers and their leaders line up on one of the eight bridges that span the Danube between Buda and Pest, and combine them into Budapest.

around the half-hidden walls built by the Turks who occupied Hungary in the 1500's.

Today Sandor goes to Buda on his own. He works on a miniature railway built by the government for the Pioneers, a Hungarian youth group. About 50 Pioneers, all under the age of 16, operate electric trains over eight miles of track, transporting passengers to the hotels and restaurants near Buda's hot springs.

Recently Sandor's Aunt Maria and Uncle Charles, who now live in the United States, came back to Hungary for a visit. They suggested that Sandor return the visit, perhaps going to school in the United States for a year.

Since then, Sandor has thought of little else. But he has doubts. It's easy for foreigners to get permission to visit Hungary. But the government disapproves of Hungarians traveling to non-Communist nations. It wants to keep Hungarian money and skills at home. And it is afraid that young people who get a taste of Western affluence will not want to return to Hungary.

Aunt Maria and Uncle Charles fled Hungary in 1956 with about 190,000 other Hungarians. That was the year when the Hungarian people revolted against the government.

Hungary, allied with the defeated Germans, had lost much of its territory after World War I. One part of Hungary was given to Czechoslovakia. Another part went to Rumania. A third part helped form the new nation of Yugoslavia. With these lands went most of Hungary's forests and its gold, silver, copper, and salt mines. Although what was left was mostly a broad and rich plain, called the Alfold, the peasants had little land. A few wealthy families owned most of it.

❧ They find new buildings rising in the cities, but there's still a housing shortage.

New housing in Budapest is likely to look much like these apartment buildings — simple, uniform, even drab — evenly spaced on treeless lots.

Between the two World Wars, Hungarians kept hoping to win back some of their lost territory. In 1939 they allied themselves with Germany's Adolf Hitler, the most powerful man in Europe, who promised to help them regain the lands.

181

But Hitler was defeated in World War II. What's more, the victorious Soviet army did not leave Hungary when the war ended. It stayed on to make sure that Hungarian Communists would be well represented in the new government.

In the 1949 elections, all the candidates for office were Communists or Communist supporters. Soon all Hungarian industries, businesses, and banks were taken over by the state. Collectivization of farms was begun.

Eva has often told her children how hard it was to find enough to eat in the years after World War II. Farmers refused to produce the food quotas the government demanded. Industries did not function well under their new government managers. They failed to meet production goals.

After Stalin died in 1953, life improved somewhat for workers and peasants. A leader named Imre Nagy* slowed the development of heavy industry and tried to control the secret police.

But the Soviets did not like Nagy's changes and they helped throw him out of office. Many Hungarians, remembering how much better life had been under Nagy, refused to accept the return of the old rule. They took their protests to the streets.

On October 23, 1956, the Hungarian secret police fired without warning into a crowd of demonstrators. They killed nearly a hundred people. Those murders triggered the revolution and the rise of the Hungarian Freedom Fighters.

For a short time it seemed that the Freedom Fighters might actually win. But the Soviet Union could not allow such a victory. Afraid other Communist countries might follow Hungary's example, it sent in Soviet troops to crush the revolution.

The fighting lasted about two weeks. Many were

182

slain, many others imprisoned. When the fighting stopped, the revolution had been crushed.

Many Hungarians who fled in 1956 have, like Uncle Charles and Aunt Maria, come back — but only to visit. They find their country changed. They sense that Hungarians support their government, but with little enthusiasm. They find new buildings rising in the cities, but there's still a housing shortage. They see heavy traffic on the Danube — barges delivering ore and timber for export, hydrofoils carrying tourists between Vienna and Budapest.

Western influences are obvious in Hungary. Girls wear short skirts and patterned stockings. Boys wear blue jeans — called "Texas" — and long hair. Almost everywhere are Coca-Cola signs. Eva's bookstore sells recent American novels and plays in translation.

The churches, although sometimes crowded, seem to be dying. Most of the congregants are old. The young people rarely attend.

"Today," says Eva, "young people here recite poetry, not prayers." In Hungary, as in the Soviet Union, poetry is popular with young people. Perhaps this is because radical protests seem to get past the censors more easily in verse. The poet-heroes of the public are those who are out of favor with the government.

"The reason that there are so many unhappy people in Hungary," jokes Eva, "is that there aren't enough publishers for all the poetry written here."

But most Hungarians are really seeking better wages, not publishers. The lure of higher-paying jobs has drawn many peasants and farmers to the cities. Some commute daily from homes in outlying villages. Some live in workers' dormitories in the cities during the week, seeing their families only on weekends.

About a third of Hungary's people are still farmers. However, most farms are now part of the collective system. And life in the country is slowly changing. For example, irrigation has come to the farmlands. Canals and wells have been dug in the Alfold, the great fertile plain that extends for hundreds of miles through central and east Hungary.

Hungarian-style cowboys, called *csikosok*,* still ride the Alfold. Wearing wide-pleated trousers, loose cloaks, and broad-brimmed hats, they keep watch over the big herds of cattle and horses bred on the Hungarian steppes.

Hungarian villages are still very poor. Most houses are low and roofed with red tile. Most have electricity, and some even have TV. But few have indoor plumbing or a refrigerator. Many roads are unpaved.

Old men sit outside their houses on good days and play *ultimo*,* a card game like bridge. Old women, dressed in black, embroider flowers on skirts and blouses. Some of them take care of little children whose parents are at work.

At the end of the week, friends often get together in the evening to talk. The livelier ones dance the *csardas*,* the national dance of Hungary. It is named after the *csarda*, the country inn where people gather.

Working in the fields, cooking, raising children — these are among the main concerns of Hungarian villagers. Their life is rooted in old, old traditions. Politics and foreign affairs are not important. Any concern with such matters died after the 1956 revolution.

"As long as one fights, one cares," says an old man sadly to a visitor from the West. "People here have given up fighting." Hanging on the wall behind the old man's chair is a motto reading, "If the earth is God's hat, Hungary is a flower on the brim."

Chapter 15

East Germany: The Other Side of the Wall

"IT'S INCREDIBLY UGLY."

"It's really up-to-date."

"It looks like a lunch box."

That's how some East Germans describe the *Konsument,** one of the country's biggest department stores. Built of gleaming aluminum without windows, the store has been a center of controversy since it opened in the city of Leipzig.* It is only one of the many attractions that have drawn people to Leipzig since it was founded more than 900 years ago.

Leipzig, like all of Germany, has a rich and ancient cultural heritage. Here are just a few of the accomplishments for which Leipzig itself is associated:

The 16th-century German monk, Martin Luther, held a famous debate on the Protestant Reformation in Leipzig in 1519.

The 17th-century German philosopher, Wilhelm von Leibniz,* and the 19th-century composer, Richard Wagner,* were both born here.

Johann Wolfgang von Goethe* (1749-1832), one of the greatest creative minds in history, was a graduate of Leipzig University.

Felix Mendelssohn,* the 19th-century composer, made Leipzig's concerts world-famous.

Here another 19th-century composer, Robert Schumann,* wrote his major works, as did Johann Sebastian Bach* (1685-1750), who was organist at the Church of St. Thomas for a quarter century.

Today Leipzig has been made a showcase for Communist East Germany. Its streets are well lighted. It has the Konsument and many smaller shops. Its bookstores and record shops are full of works by both West and East Germans.

A high point of life today is the annual Leipzig Trade Fair. Established more than 800 years ago, this is the oldest trade fair in Europe. The Leipzig Trade Fair displays the goods of thousands of exhibitors from more than 80 countries.

Defeated in World War II, Germany was split into the Federal Republic of Germany (West) and the German Democratic Republic (East). Germany, however, had been divided before. In fact, during the 1700's, Germany was only a geographical name for some 300 independent German states. It took a business arrangement to begin to bring these states together. In 1834 many of the states formed a customs union. This paved the way for their eventual political union.

The customs union was a good example of how businessmen can sometimes lead politicians. For the customs union cut down or cut out the taxes on goods traded among the German states. It made buying and selling easier and more profitable.

With that start, all of Germany was brought together in 1871 under the leadership of Otto von

Leipzig is both a historic city and a modern international trade center. These traffic controllers are busy routing trolleys and trains around Leipzig's Plaza of the Republic.

Bismarck.* He was the prime minister of Prussia, biggest of the old German states. He accomplished the unification of Germany through a militant policy, which he called "blood and iron." At the same time, Bismarck involved his people in wars against his neighbors. He went to war against France — the Franco-Prussian War of 1871 — and won a convincing victory. Germany took territory that lay between the two countries.

Nearly half a century later, in 1914, Germany went to war once more against its old foe, France. In World War I (1914-18), however, Germany was badly beaten. Its ruler, Kaiser Wilhelm,* went into exile, and its economy fell into ruins. Bewildered and hungry, Germany was ripe for a "strong man."

In the 1920's that strong man appeared. Adolf Hitler and his new National Socialist (Nazi) Party began to gain popularity. Hitler came to power in the election of 1933. Soon the whole of Germany was taking orders from the Nazis. The government was Hitler's rubber stamp. Business, education, youth, sports, entertainment, the communications media — every part of German life was under Hitler's thumb.

Conquest was Hitler's goal, the conquest of all Europe — and perhaps the world. If he could do so by bluff and the show of force, fine. If he had to make war in order to conquer territory, he was ready to do so. Czechoslovakia fell to the Nazis by the threat of attack in 1938 (see Chapter 13). Hitler's armies marched into Poland in September 1939 (see Chapter 12), and World War II started.

In 1945 World War II ended in Europe with the death of Hitler and the destruction of the Nazi state. The Soviet forces had driven into the eastern part of Germany. The Western Allies — the United States, Britain, and France — each occupied a section of Western Germany. The city of Berlin was divided between the Communists and the non-Communist powers.

Under their occupation forces, West Germany and West Berlin began to revive and rebuild. But East Germany and East Berlin failed to progress. Like those in West Germany, East German factories had

188

⋖§ That scar is the Berlin Wall, a real wall of concrete and barbed wire, patrolled by East German armed guards.

Why was the Berlin Wall built? Whom does it lock in? Whom does it keep out? Why must Berlin be split down the middle? Why must all of Germany be divided into East and West?

been pounded into rubble. East German farms had been torn by bombing and shelling. The Soviet Union, its own factories and farms in ruins, was unable to help much.

Jealous of West Germany's revival, the Soviets

were determined to drive the Western Allies out of West Berlin. In 1948 the Soviet forces blockaded the road, rail, and water routes from West Germany to West Berlin. They hoped to make West Berlin knuckle under to communism. But the Western Allies mounted a mammoth airlift operation. The blockade was finally lifted in 1949.

That same year the Western Allies removed their controls from West Germany and allowed it to become the independent Federal Republic of Germany. West Berlin is included as a city and a state in West Germany, but its government is still under the control of the Western Allies.

In 1949 as well, the Soviet authorities permitted the East Germans to set up the German Democratic Republic. But the Soviet Union still strongly influences every move that East Germany makes.

East Berlin is the capital of East Germany. It is at last recovering from the wounds of World War II. But it still bears a scar, self-inflicted in 1961. That scar is the Berlin Wall, a real wall of concrete and barbed wire, patrolled by East German armed guards. First set up between East and West Berlin, the wall was extended to block the whole border between East and West Germany.

The Berlin Wall was built to halt the flight of East Germans to West Berlin. Thousands were leaving every day, running to freedom in West Berlin, West Germany, other places in Western Europe, or even the Americas. Today most visitors from the West are permitted to cross the Wall to see friends or do business in East Germany. But few East Germans are ever allowed to cross over into the West.

Klaus* and Dagmar* are two East Berliners who are content to stay on their side of the Berlin Wall. They live in a new three-room apartment on the

The tall building in the background, a cultural center, was designed by this young woman architect. East Germany is educating women for the professions and giving them a chance to use their skills.

Karl Marx Allee.* This street is one of the busiest and most fashionable boulevards in East Berlin.

Klaus has helped design several new buildings in East Berlin. He is an architect, working for the East German government in the Ministry of Architecture. Dagmar is a free-lance photographer. Together they earn about $800 a month, which is a high income in

East Germany. It puts Klaus and Dagmar in a new wealthy class.

Some members of this wealthy class are also members of the Communist Party. Klaus and Dagmar belong to the Party. Many other prosperous East Germans are not at all interested in politics. They have made a comfortable life for themselves without joining the Party. In fact, only one in five adults belongs to the Party.

Rudi, the only child of Klaus and Dagmar, lived with his grandmother for the first five years of his life because there wasn't room for him in his parents' old apartment. Now 10, he has a room of his own — but he must share it with his father's drawing board, his mother's photography gear, and a dining table.

Although Klaus likes ordinary German food — *wurst* (sausage), beef stew, spiced pork, vinegar pickles, herring, layer cakes — he also likes hard-to-obtain imported foods.

Dagmar disapproves of her husband's food extravagances, but she too has an expensive habit. Every year she buys two or three expensive dresses designed by one of East Germany's few top dressmakers. Aside from these designs, most men's and women's clothes in East Germany are years behind Western styles.

Stylish clothing and gourmet foods may be out of reach for most East Germans today. But good entertainment is not. Movies, including some from Western countries, are plentiful. The Berliner Ensemble, founded by playwright Bertolt Brecht,* is now a successful theater group. It performs to enthusiastic audiences all over East Germany. The *Komische Oper** (Comic Opera) is considered East Germany's finest cultural offering.

Vacations are inexpensive in East Germany. Here, as in other Communist countries, most of the holiday costs are paid for by the company that employs the worker. Since most of the companies are government-owned, it is really the state that foots the bill for travel and relaxation.

Dagmar, Klaus, and Rudi plan to vacation at a resort on the Baltic Sea this year. Rudi is looking forward to traveling by train to the port of Rostock. Rostock calls itself the "Gateway to the World," even though East Germans are not allowed to travel to non-Communist lands. In the Middle Ages, it was an important trading port.

East German architects have restored some of the medieval flavor of Rostock. New buildings have been erected to blend in with the traditional red-brick houses with tall sloping roofs. Klaus is eager to study these new houses and see how they fit in with the work he is doing.

What Rudi will do when he grows up depends on the future of East Germany itself. From a slow start after World War II, it has made great technical progress. It has built housing and industry. It has established a good national system of free schools.

But many East Germans find it hard to live without greater personal freedoms. Students complain that they don't have enough choice in their courses of study. Musicians complain that the only music the government will approve of are "marches that help build socialism" or "songs suitable for a worker chorus." Newspaper readers complain that there's no world news in the government-run papers.

Once the East Germans did revolt against their government. In 1953 a bloodless uprising was quickly put down by Soviet troops and tanks. Today there is little protest, either open or underground. The average East German may be unenthusiastic about communism, but he or she is learning to live with it.

193